The American Mind In the Age of Trump

God versus Secularism
✑
Capitalism versus Capitalistic-Socialism

By
Ivan Beggs

For permission requests, write to the publisher:

Quest4A@protonmail.com

Ivanbeggs.com

"The American Mind in the Age of Trump" by Ivan Beggs

Editor: Jim Nelson, Hendersonville, NC

Book Design: Phyllis Barnard, Candler, NC

Cover Design: Phyllis Barnard – Candler, NC

ISBN: 978-1-7341167-3-1 Soft cover – black & white - English

ISBN: 978-1-7341167-4-8 Soft cover – black & white - German

POL040000   POLITICAL SCIENCE / American Government / General

POL046000   POLITICAL SCIENCE / Commentary & Opinion

POL042000   POLITICAL SCIENCE / Political Ideologies / General

p. cm.

HF0000.A0 A00 2010

299.000 00–dc22 2010999999

First Edition

14 13 12 11 10 / 10 9 8 7 6 5 4 3 2 1

Dedication

Many thanks to Marlene, my wife for fifty years, for her patience and especially my children. Many thanks to the hundreds and hundreds of people who shared the thoughts and concerns about God, secularism, capitalism, and socialism with me.

A special thank you to Irene Baltes for inspiring the book from a German perspective.

Please send comments for discussion and to improve the book to:

Quest4a@protonmail.com

Ivanbeggs.com

Books by Ivan Beggs

Quest for a Meaningful Life through Christianity, Judaism, Islam, Buddhism, and Hinduism

Fourteen Doubts About Five Religions: An Exploration of Christianity, Judaism, Islam, Buddhism, and Hinduism

CONTENTS

Introduction

Upon the founding of the United States of America in 1776, the Continental Congress adopted three mottos. They were a statement to the new nation and the world.

Out of many, one – E pluribus unum[1]

A new order of the ages – Novus ordo seclorum[2]

Providence favors our undertaking – Annuit Coeptis.[3]

Then in 1956 during the great atheistic Communist scare, President and General of the Army Dwight David Eisenhower, with agreement from the US Congress, made the official motto to be

In God We Trust[4]

There is a fundamental understanding in these four mottos. The first three say that Providence, a nebulous term for a divine force, blesses a new nation created out of many people[5] as the new order for the ages. However, because the US was fighting Godless Communism, and for all the American people to understand, the new motto was written in simple English. Conservative Churches strongly supported the change to, "In God We Trust." Thus, discreetly sidelining the first three mottos which were written in Latin and unintelligible to most Americans.

The other strong force is capitalism versus socialism. From the 1500's to the early 1900's, the US was very independent, entrepreneurial, and capitalistic. As the society became more complex and interdependent concerns grew for the wellbeing of the entire nation. People became aware that the primary reason for the Constitution as stated in its Preamble is, "to provide for the

---

1   (Wikipedia - E pluribus unum 2020)

2   (Wikipedia - Novus ordo seclorum 2020)

3   (Wikipedia - Annuit coeptis 2020)

4   (Wikipedia - In God We Trust 2020)

5   Some feel that "many" really means "The Thirteen Colonies" and not a sly reference to 'many diverse people' as thought of today. Interesting how diverse people make interpretations.

general welfare." Thus, President Franklin Roosevelt created the New Deal during the Great Depression. However, many considered the New Deal to be socialism that would make the US like Communist Russia and would weaken the core economic strength of the US.

Thus, this book in nine chapters explains two powerful tensions in the American Mind:

God versus Secularism and

Capitalism versus Capitalistic-Socialism

In the Age of Trump

Chapter 1

Freedom

Diverse populations seeking freedom and wealth

Approximately 10,000 to 20,000 years ago, Native Americans began settling in what is now the Continental United States. Estimates of their population around the time of Columbus in 1492, vary wildly from 3 million to 18 million to 112 million. By 1890 their population declined to 250,000 due to disease and genocide. Currently, their population is about 3 million.[6]

Prior to Columbus finding the New World in 1492, the American continents were free of the European influence until the 1500's. Then wealth, land, and power seekers such as the Spanish, Portuguese, British, Dutch, and French nations along with Catholic and Protestant clergy brutally conquered the new lands in North, Central, and South America.

By the early 1700's the East Coast was 80% English and 20% slaves. Most of the slaves were in the Southern area.

At the time of the American Revolution the English were 50% of the population, slaves 20%, Scotch-Irish 8%, German 7%, Scots 7%, and Dutch 3%.

Then millions of people came seeking freedom from the European masters, wanting new opportunities, a chance for land, and some wealth. Those that could not afford the passage agreed to work for someone who paid their way–often for seven years as indentured servants. Other Europeans came as part of colonial armies and stayed when their armies went home.

Approximately 400,000 slaves came to the US and 7,300,000 to the Caribbean, Central America, and South America. About 10-15% died in the brutal passage.[7]

---

6   (Wikipedia - Native Americans in the United States 2020)

7   (Buchholz 2019)

In 2017, 45 million people living in the U.S. were born in another country, accounting for about one-fifth of the world's migrants in 2017. They are from just about every country in the world. 35 million are lawful and 11 million are illegal.[8] Demographers project that the foreign-born population will reach 78 million by 2065.

60% of the US views immigration as a strength and 30% as a burden.[9] Those who view immigrants as a burden make the most political noise.

The 2010 Census shows where the number of current immigrants came from:

16,000,000	Latin America
3,000,000	Northern Europe
3,000,000	Western Europe (800,000 from Russia)
3,000,000	Southern Europe
3,000,000	Eastern Europe (800,000 from Russia)
8,000,000	Asia
900,000	Africa
800,000	Canada
37,600,000[10]	Total current immigrants

Next is a chart showing where Americans claimed heritage from and the size of that country:

---

8   (Pew Research Center - Jynnah Radford 2019)

9   (Pew Research Center - Jynnah Radford 2019)

10   Totals in the paragraphs vary slightly based on sources. The point is, the US has a diverse ethnic population.

Heritage Claim	Claimed US Heritage	Population of Country Claimed
Hispanic	52,500,000[11]	600,000,000[12]
English	49,600,000[13]	67,000,000[14]
German	49,800,000[15]	84,000,000[16]
African	44,000,000[17]	1,300,000,000[18]
Scotch-Irish	33,000,000[19]	7,000,000[20]
Italian	16,000,000[21]	60,000,000[22]
Native American	3,000,000[23]	18,000,000 to 112,000,000[24]

Note that the African American population grew from 400,000[25] during slave times to 44,000,000 as of 2019.[26]

With a population approximately 328,000,000, the US is about 72% white,

---

11   (US Census Bureau - Quick Facts n.d.) US population estimate 328,000,000 with 16% Hispanic is 52,500,000 Hispanic.

12   (World Population Review - Central America and South America 2020)

13   (Wikipedia - English Americans 2020)

14   (Worldometer 2020)

15   (Wikipedia - German American 2020)

16   (Macrotrends 2020)

17   (US Census Bureau - Quick Facts n.d.) US population estimate 328,000,000 with 13.4% black is 44,000,000 African American.

18   (World Populatioin Review - Africa 2020)

19   (Wikipedia - English Americans 2020)

20   (Wikipedia - Irish Americans 2020)

21   (OSIA - Italian Americans in the US 2004)

22   (Worldometer - Population of Italy 2020)

23   (Wikipedia - Native Americans in the United States 2020)

24   The population numbers vary widely in various sources. Who knows which is evenly roughly accurate?

25   (Buchholz 2019)

26   (US Census Bureau - Quick Facts n.d.) US population estimate 328,000,000 with 13.4% black is 44,000,000 black or African American.

16% Hispanic, 13% African American, 5% Asian, and Native American 1%.[27]

Thus, the US population is one of the most ethnically diverse countries in the world. That diversity is both a strength and an issue that politicians and various groups have since the formation of the US have manipulated for personal gain while others have tried to form a more powerful union.

Manifest Destiny – "This Land is Our Land"

In the early 1800's, "Manifest Destiny" was a widely held cultural belief that its settlers were destined to expand across North America. For many there was an enthusiasm to head West for opportunity, to get land, and to create one's destiny. The feeling permeated the air. There are three basic themes to Manifest Destiny:

- The special virtues of the American people and their institutions
- The mission of the United States to redeem and remake the West in the image of agrarian America
- An irresistible destiny to carry out this essential duty[28]

Thus, the creation of one nation from the Atlantic to the Pacific was the American destiny in the 18th and 19th Centuries. In an immensely popular song in 1956, Woody Guthrie captured that feeling:

> This land is your land, this land is my land
> From the California, to the New York Island
> From the Redwood Forest, to the Gulf stream waters
> This land was made for you and me[29]

There was a feeling that it was destiny to form a nation and that President James Monroe declared in 1823 that "… that any intervention by external powers in the politics of the North, Central, and South Americas is a

27   (Wikipedia - Racial and ethnic categories 2020)

28   (Wikipedia - Manifest Destiny 2020)

29   (Guthrie 1956 (renewed), 1958 (renewed), 1970, and 1972)

potentially hostile act against the US." In 1850 people began to call it the Monroe Doctrine.[30]

However, as with all societies and especially in the US, not all agreed with Manifest Destiny nor the Monroe Doctrine. There were many who labored in squalid factories and lived in shabby tenements. Still, the culture basically embraced both. More immigrants came to the US seeking their opportunity or least an escape from the old oppressive European societal and legal structures.

Freedom vs authority

The American experience created a new person. Someone that had no master and was not a slave. The very air and circumstances created a new person that was free and independent. Benjamin Franklin and others would agree with J. Hector St. John de Crèvecœur's clear statement:

> (The American is neither) European or the descendant of an European, hence that strange mixture of blood, which you will find in no other country. I could point out to you a family whose grandfather was an Englishman, whose wife was Dutch, whose son married a French woman, and whose present four sons have now four wives of different nations. *He* is an American, who leaving behind him all his ancient prejudices and manners, receives new ones from the new mode of life he has embraced, the new government he obeys, and the new rank he holds. He becomes an American by being received in the broad lap of our great *Alma Mater.*

> Here individuals of all nations are melted into a new race of men, whose labors and posterity will one day cause great changes in the world. Americans are the western pilgrims, who are carrying along with them that great mass of arts, sciences, vigor, and industry which began long since in the East; they will finish the great circle.

---

30   (Wikipedia - Monroe Doctrine 2020)

The Americans were once scattered all over Europe; here they are incorporated into one of the finest systems of population which has ever appeared, and which will hereafter become distinct by the power of the different climates they inhabit. The American ought therefore to love this country much better than that wherein either he or his forefathers were born.

Here the rewards of his industry follow with equal steps the progress of his labor; his labor is founded on the basis of nature, *self-interest;* can it want a stronger allurement? Wives and children, who before in vain demanded of him a morsel of bread, now fat and frolicsome, gladly help their father to clear those fields whence exuberant crops are to arise to feed and to clothe them all; without any part being claimed, either by a despotic prince, a rich abbot, or a mighty lord.

Here religion demands but little of him; a small voluntary salary to the minister, and gratitude to God; can he refuse these?

The American is a new man, who acts upon new principles; he must therefore entertain new ideas and form new opinions. From involuntary idleness, servile dependence, penury, and useless labor, he has passed to toils of a very different nature, rewarded by ample subsistence;

"This is an American." [31]

It is that image that many Americans feel in their very bones when they proclaim 'freedom.' That they are free from a master. Free to live as they please without interference from neighbor, city, state, country, or foreign power. It is in the very blood and bones of many Americans.

**One is free to be free and
strive to be prosperous or
be lazy, starve, and die.**

---

31   (Susan C. Imbarrato (Crèvecoeur 1782 (Ref 2015))

It is the sense of the rugged individual, which appeared in the tough cowboy Marlboro Cigarette ads. It is typical in many movies. It is distinctly different from the European mindset.

However, while these feelings are now particularly prevalent in rural areas and less so in the urban areas, nevertheless it does permeate throughout the US. Thus,

Leave me alone to do what I want

became a core foundation in the US Constitution.

When traveling the US away from the major metropolitan areas like New York City, Los Angeles, Chicago, Cleveland, etc. there is a feeling that the rest of the world does not exit. That the concerns of Europe, Asia, Africa, Central and South America don't exist, except as a threat to personal and national security, jobs, and racial purity. That almost indescribable sense of freedom is part of the American heritage of "Leave me alone" and "I will do what I want when I want." It leads easily to isolationism. Perhaps a popular 1976 love song, "Let the world go away"[32] fits the US. Being a world citizen is not built into the American culture.

That sense fits many immigrants from the 1500's until the early 1800's as they lived alone on desolate farms, small villages, and were responsible for their own security against Native Americans, wars with foreign powers, and fending off corrupt people. Also, they raised their own food, hunted, and killed pesky creatures that ate the livestock and crops. Consequently, guns were a vital and very acceptable part of their culture. Because the guns were so prevalent, many Americans were available, figuratively speaking at, "A Minute's Notice" to form a militia to fight whatever the larger threat was. Thus, a well know picture of the, "Minute Man." A true patriot that is always ready to fight for freedom for himself, family, state, and the US. That is why the 2nd Amendment to the Constitution has gun ownership as a fundamental

---

32   (Wikipedia - T.T Ross - "Let the World Go Away" 2020)

right. A view deeply held by many, but not all Americans.

So, the idea of freedom – Freedom of speech. Freedom of the press. Freedom of assembly. Freedom from tyranny – and the right to own guns – are built into the very fiber and structure of the US Constitution.

Chapter 2

US Constitution

Declaration of Independence 1776

Every American knows two dates: July 4, 1776 and December 7, 1941. They are burned into the memory of every US student, adult, and immigrant. Anyone that does not know those two dates are not an American. There are many books and films about both events as fact and as myth.

Essentially, the Declaration of Independence said that the King of England trampled upon its' American Colonies, and thus the Colonies are justified to declare independence of the King and England.

Formation of Constitution 1789

Prior to the US Constitution, "The Articles of Confederation" was the back-bone of the US legal system. Each State[33] would "enter into a firm league of friendship with each other, for their common defense, the security of their liberties, and their mutual and general welfare."[34]

After the experience with the British Crown, the States had a deep-seated fear of a centralized government. Consequently, the federal government could print money (though without the power of taxation, the money was worthless – each state printed its own money). It could declare war with the consent of the states. Each state had one vote; but the large states resented the power of the small states to curtail the desires of states with larger populations. Individual States controlled slavery laws and customs as "The Peculiar

---

33   State is purposefully capitalized throughout the book to emphasize not a nebulous term "state" but rather the individual State such North Carolina, Massachusetts, etc. have power and that creates a tension between the States and the Federal Government.

34   (Blitz 2013)

Institution" of the South.[35]   Interstate commerce had conflicts over taxes, value of currency, limitations on the amount of goods that could pass. The States held any power not specifically granted to the Congress. Also, there was no President of the US nor Supreme Court. Thus, the States would argue among themselves to resolve disputes. At times there was a threat of civil war.[36]

Recognizing these issues, the Philadelphia Convention in May 1787 began to revise the Articles of Confederation. Today that revision is known as the US Constitution. It attempted to balance centralized vs decentralize power, small states vs large states' rights, solving disputes between the states and citizens, slavery, interstate commerce, overall leadership of the US, raising an Army for the mutual defense, ability to tax, a checks and balance system between small states, large states, the executive branch, and the Supreme Court. The new Constitution became official on March 4, 1789. Furthermore, the States adopted Ten Amendments on December 15, 1791.[37] It is difficult to imagine in today's polarized political climate creating and signing that same Constitution.

Yet unknown to most Americans, more than thirteen difficult years passed from the creation, adoption of the Declaration of Independence, to the implementation of the US Constitution. Those issues that led to the creation of the Constitution still permeate the American political system today. The key ones are Federalism[38] vs States' rights, freedom of speech, and interpreting the Constitution as originalist or a living document. The right to bear arms is in Chapter 7.

---

35   (U.S. History - The Peculiar Instution 2019)

36   (Blitz 2013)

37   (This Day in History(?) n.d.)

38   Federalism is also capitalized throughout the book to emphasize the tension between the Federal government's powers and the States' rights. It is a theme that is deeply embedded prior to the Revolution, in the US history, and is continues to be strong today.

Federalism v States Rights

At the heart of Declaration of Independence and the US Constitution is the simple yet complicated concept of freedom. How do individuals, cities, states, and the federal government exercise freedom? Today it is still a tension. What are the limits to each level of freedom? In Communist and socialist countries, the federal government has virtually unlimited freedom. The nation is supreme and determines what individuals, cities, and states can and cannot do.

However, at the heart of creating the US was the wild frontier. Starting in the 1600's settlers came to the East Coast of the US and setup their own governments mostly free of the English, Dutch, Spanish, and French monarchies. Individuals on their own headed west setting up their own individual farms and in other cases communities. For the most part no one ruled over them. Essentially, they were free from outside interference.

Though as more immigrants arrived along the East Coast, cities grew along with the needs to create mundane rules. Nevertheless, the individuals, communities, and cities were mostly independent. Those that wanted more freedom headed across the Allegheny Mountains to create freedom for themselves as individuals or as small communities. There they came into conflict with Native Indians and with the French who claimed the territory from Canada down through the Mississippi River Valley to New Orleans. Eventually the British won the French and Indian Wars claiming the region as British.

In part to pay for winning the war, the British Crown levied taxes on the American Colonies and based British troops in American homes. Some Americans accepted and others rejected the British actions. Slogans and flags appeared in favor of freedom from the Crown of England. The most famous being, "Don't Tread on Me." In essence, many colonists just wanted to live their own lives without interference from government, especially an uncaring government an ocean away that viewed Americans as second-class citizens that paid tribute to the Crown.

That desire to be free of a higher government and yet needing a government to coordinate individuals was and continues to today as a fundamental tension. It appears in the US Constitution. "The powers not delegated to the United States by the Constitution, nor prohibited by it to the States, are reserved to the States respectively, or to the people." [39] Simply stated it is Federalism vs States' Rights.

That tension appeared the strongest with the American Civil War and afterwards into the 1960's and continues to today known as "States' Rights". It was a code that each State has the right to decide if there will be slavery, how to treat minorities, determine who can and cannot vote, what if any environmental protection laws to have, whether creationism or Darwinism will be taught in schools, what type of taxes to levy, what rights women and minorities could have, etc. One father felt so strongly about it, that he named one of his sons, "States Rights Gist".[40]

States' Rights is so strong of an issue that in the 2016 Presidential Campaign thirteen Republican contenders made various statements that they would downsize the overreaching bloated federal government by eliminating the Environmental Protection Agency, Department of Education, the Commerce Department, Education Department, Interior Department, Housing and Urban Development Department, Transportation Department, Agriculture Department, Labor Department, Homeland Security Department, Council of Economic Advisors, and the Small Business Administration,[41] as well as the Office of Personnel Management.

The actions continue in a variety of forms. For example, move agencies from

---

39   Passed by Congress September 25, 1789. Ratified December 15, 1791 as the Tenth Amendment.

40   (Richard W. Hatcher III - South Carolina Encyclopedia - "States Rights Gist" 2016)

41   (Jason Plautz - How to Eliminate Almost Every Federal Agency 2014)

Washington, DC to other parts of the country to be closer to the people.[42] Thus, without approval from Congress, eliminating many staffers who would not move and reducing the power and expertise of the agency. Another is for every rule or law instituted Congress and the agency must eliminate two to ten other rules or laws.[43] Another way is that if Congress approves funding for an agency, the Department head or the President will not authorize spending the funds.[44] With all that and other noise going on, a key drive is to abolish federal and local State inheritance taxes.[45]

Essentially, the idea is that the States understand better how to manage the funds than the federal government does. Therefore, have the States spend the money. One form is for the federal government to give the States block grants which the States will spend as they see fit. Or as one briefly popular commentator quipped, "Make the federal government so small you can flush it down the toilette."[46]

Freedom of Speech

A core of the American psyche is being free to say what one wants to say. That one can express an opinion without government interference. Thus, the Constitution states,

> Congress shall make no law respecting an establishment of religion, or prohibiting the free exercise thereof; or abridging the freedom of speech, or of the press; or the right of the people peaceably to assemble,

---

42   (Jason Plautz - How to Eliminate Almost Every Federal Agency 2014)

43   (NOLAN D. MCCASKILL and MATTHEW NUSSBAUM - Trump signs executive order requiring that for every one new regulation, two must be revoked 2017)

44   (Ted Johnson - Donald Trump Again Wants To Eliminate Funding For Public Media, But Congress Likely Won't Let Him 2020)

45   (Naomi Jagoda - Senate Republicans reintroduce bill to repeal the estate tax 2019)

46   (Wikiquote - Grover Norquist 2019)

and to petition the Government for a redress of grievances.[47]

At first glance it is a simple and straight forward statement about freedom of expression. As with anything, the Devil is in the details…

A core issue today is how much religious freedom is allowed. Some people say anyone can have a 'deeply held religious belief' to not do certain tasks. Here are some examples.

Not serve in the military because one's religion is against violence and war. However, one must pay taxes to support the military establishment and wars.

Not perform abortion, nor provide nor touch any form of prophylaxis because of religious grounds.

Permit a baker to not serve a gay couple because the religion considers homosexuality a sin; or permit a person to refuse renting an apartment or perform other services to homosexuals.

Make pornographic material illegal or allow a clerk to not handle objectionable material because of religious reasons.

Demand to have Creationism instead of evolution taught in schools or at least to have both taught as being valid.

To have prayer at the beginning of public events such as sporting events, school board meetings, city, county, state, and federal government meetings.

One side is in favor of unlimited religious freedom in public areas. That the separation of church and state means the state cannot dictate what churches and their members cannot do. That they have their religious freedom to act in accordance with their beliefs. Also, that religious have the right to have their beliefs and laws become the law of the land.

---

47   First Amendment to the U.S. Constitution

The other side fights a losing battle that there is a separation of church and state, meaning that religion cannot interfere with the freedom of citizens. That there is no religious test for office. That religion is a private matter.

Freedom of speech means that a person can say whatever they wish, whenever they wish, wherever they wish. However, the courts have ruled that there are limits on that speech. One cannot create riot such as falsely yell at a movie theater fire. Hate speech is prohibited. However, speech against others might not be considered hate speech if it is a deeply held religious speech. False statements against people are not allowed unless that person is a public figure.

On the one hand the Constitution does allow freedom of speech and the press for extremists and conspiracy views. But how far? At what point are those views curtailed? Do people have a right to not quarantine themselves in their homes when the government says to for the general health of the public? After all, they have the right to assembly, to protest, and to make their views known. This includes going to religious events during a lock-down. Or does it?

At what point will the US Government limit total free speech on the Internet to protect the public from what it or someone determines to be hateful, wrong, or creating violence? These are issues that the Congress and the courts have yet to work out.

Originalist or Living Document?

There are two main ways of interpreting the US Constitution: The Originalist and as a Living Document.

Originalist interpretation of the US Constitution means interpreting it as the signers meant it and not as people would like it to be today. If one wants a different interpretation, then go through the process of making the change which is intentionally laborious. The writers of the Constitution did not want the Constitution easily changed. There had to be serious reasons that the American society must agree to have the change.

So, to make a change one must convince the US Congress that the change is necessary and widely supported. Then the Congress can submit a proposed constitutional amendment to the states if the proposed change of language is approved with two thirds of the votes of the two chambers. Or, Congress must convene a convention to propose a change by two-thirds of the states (i.e. 34 out of 50 states).

For example, an Amendment was started in 1972 to enshrine equal rights to women in the US Constitution. It simply states, "Equality of rights under the law shall not be denied or abridged by the United States or by any state on account of sex." It seeks to, "…guarantee equal legal rights for all American citizens regardless of sex. It seeks to end the legal distinctions between men and women in terms of divorce, property, employment, and other matters." That Amendment is still not legally ratified nearly fifty years later.

On the other hand, the interpretation as a living document means that the writers and signers had a different worldview than today. Therefore, interpret the US constitution for today's understanding and issues. For example, opponents of the ERA state that there are plenty of laws that guarantee the rights of women eliminating the need for passing the ERA. Those laws are used by Originalists against the ERA. They are concerned that in the future the living document interpretation of the ERA will mean that the definition of sex will be redefined to include abhorrent groups, like LGBTQ, and possibly others. Which would diminish their "deeply held religious beliefs.

Although not specifically mentioned in the Constitution, Corporations are becoming increasingly powerful in the American political life.

Chapter 3

Corporations

Creation of a Vast Middle Class

In the later 1800's and through the 1900's, the US created wealth for millions of Americans and people in other countries that historically was unimaginable. American ingenuity coupled with corporations mass produced farming equipment, refrigerators, cars, cameras, light bulbs, electrical generation and distribution systems, ships, armaments, medical equipment, education systems, health systems, insurance, magazines, newspapers, radio, television, satellites, cell phones, computers, paper, pens, etc. Never in world history has such a rapid creation of wealth occurred for the average person in such a short period of time.

The efforts created a prosperous middle class. With the right job, a man could go to work and raise a family while the wife stayed home. After thirty or forty years he and the wife could retire relatively comfortably with a pension, Social Security, and Medicare. Though today both partners must work to make a passable living and are frequently one paycheck away from the American version of poverty. Still, in general Americans along with many others in the world are living better than any other generation in the history of the world.

This creation of wealth is due in part to individual ingenuity, social concerns, and especially the capitalistic enterprise of banking and manufacturing corporations.

Working Conditions

However, while the massive transformation occurred in less than one-hundred and fifty years, large groups of people struggled in unhealthy and unsafe working conditions six days a week, ten, twelve, and more hours per day for mediocre pay and lived in abysmal tenement housing. Early on, companies calculated the pay for a man was fifty percent of a living wage. For the woman it was twenty-five percent of a living wage. For each child it was twelve percent of a living wage. Thus, if the whole family worked then they could live, yet not prosper. However, after World War II, the situation changed, and a vibrant middle class arose.

But in the past fifty years the middle-class wealth has been disappearing to the upper classes and to developing countries. Yet, the middle class has more entertainment, food, medical care, cars, toys, and creature comforts than any society in human civilization. Yet, vast numbers of the middle class feel left behind. How can that be?

Unions

To improve these conditions, organized labor unions fought for better wages, reasonable hours, and safer working conditions. They campaigned to stop child labor, have health benefits, and take care of injured workers, and have retirement benefits.[48] Their impact, along with the productivity of corporations dramatically improved the lives of millions.

However, after the gains were achieved by the 1950's, unions tended to lose their ways with corruption and meaningless strikes which hampered US international competitiveness. As a result, dogged efforts by corporations and political opposition, offshoring of production, massive influx of foreign goods, moving production from the union friendly Northern States to the non-union States, and Ronald Reagan's anti-union stance, along with corruption and ineptness of labor leadership, union membership declined from about fifty percent to less than seventeen percent. Forces are still at work to destroy unions as an economic and political force.[49] Many workers today resent paying union dues for what they perceive as little benefits.

---

48   (History - Labor Movement 2020)

49   (History - Labor Movement 2020)

Corporate Rights and Corporations as Individuals

By the mid-1970's corporations became more aware of the power of unions, and liberals were writing laws and rules that adversely affected corporate freedom of action. They decided, "To have a place at the table and to write the rules. If we are not at the table, someone else will write the rules and eat our lunch. We must be at the table. That means getting involved in politics."[50] Several relatively subtle yet powerful forces were created: The American Legislative Exchange Council, lobbyists, and US Supreme Court decisions.

As a result, corporations formed in-house sections to work with legislatures to craft more business-friendly laws and support organizations that were friendly to businesses. One such group, American Legislative Exchange Council (ALEC), focused on drafting model legislation for the fifty state governments and the federal government. The aim is, "… dedicated to the principles of limited government, free markets and federalism. Comprised of nearly one-quarter of the country's state legislators and stakeholders from across the policy spectrum, ALEC members represent more than 60 million Americans and provide jobs to more than 30 million people in the United States." [51] It is composed of both businesses, State, and federal legislators.

ALEC writes model legislation in fiscal discipline, federalism and international relations, health and human services, Homeland Security, free speech, innovation and technology, balance of government, civil justice, commercial activities, criminal justice, education and workforce development, energy-environment-agriculture, taxes and fiscal policy, and other areas as appropriate.[52] While its scope is broad its reach goes to the federal, state, and county governments. Thus, the well thought out model legislature saves the various government entities time, money, and effort. It also creates a strong business friendly environment.

---

50   A common statement or sentiment by Chairmen of corporations.

51   (ALEC - American Legislative Exchange Council n.d.)

52   (ALEC - American Legislative Exchange Council n.d.)

Then the US Supreme Court made several rulings stating that corporations are people. Thus, they have political rights to free speech in politics and can have make decisions based upon deeply held religious beliefs that do not agree with federal, state, nor county laws. They can back legislation that the shareholders do not agree with and are unable to muster the funds to persuade millions of other shareholders to object. The corporations can also back business friendly political candidates.[53]

With these two forces in the background, the most visible force has been political lobbyists and Political Action Committees.

Political Action Committees (PAC's)

Businesses, labor, or ideological groups that raise and spend money to elect and defeat candidates are legally named Political Action Committees (PAC's). There are financial limits on spending money.[54]

In 2010, Congress created a new type of PAC. They make no contributions to candidates or parties. They run ads, send mail, support radio and TV programs, with messages that specifically advocate the election or defeat of a specific candidate. There are no limits or restrictions on the sources of funds for these expenditures.[55] Corporations began very naturally funding these super-PACS.

The US Supreme Court said that corporations are people for freedom of speech purposes. As a result, corporations had the full rights to spend money as they wish in candidate elections — federal, state, and local. The decision reversed a century of legal understanding, unleashed a flood of campaign

53   (Ciara Torres-Spelliscy - "American Bar Association" n.d.)

54   (OpenSecrets - What is a PAC? n.d.) Most PACs represent business, labor or ideological interests. PACs can give $5,000 to a candidate committee per election (primary, general or special). They can also give up to $15,000 annually to any national party committee, and $5,000 annually to any other PAC. PACs may receive up to $5,000 from any one individual, PAC or party committee per calendar year.

55   (OpenSecrets - What is a PAC? n.d.)

cash and created a crescendo of controversy that continues to build today.[56]

Thus today, corporations with or without PAC's can spend virtually unlimited amounts of money on political election campaigns and influence political legislation. The result is that corporations have a greater influence upon the political process than in the past 250 years. So much so that some pundits claim that the US is becoming fascist – that is the corporations run the US for the benefit of corporations.

In turn conservative churches are beginning to exercise their political freedoms in election campaigns and making of laws. Some fear this is moving he country towards a Conservative Christian theocracy. As they partner more with the corporations, there are concerns that the US will be run by corporations and conservative Christian clergy.

In general, corporations along with other groups have quietly been dismantling Franklin D. Roosevelt's New Deal of the 1930's.

Cutting Taxes

There is the "Trickle Down Economics." That cutting taxes on corporations and the wealthy will stimulate the economy and thus the benefits will 'trickle' down' to the average people. Thus, Republicans cut taxes as much as is politically possible. On the other hand, Democrats point out that most of the benefits go to the corporations and the top five percent of the population while the rest of the country gets very little benefit. That is, 'only a trickle reached the average people.

Social Security and Medicare taxes are 7.65% on corporate/business payroll and 7.65% on individual earnings for a total of 15.3%. In general corporations want to be free of contributing their portion of that tax. The burden to funding would then be placed upon the individual worker. Additionally, various schemes are considered such as making SS & Medicare to be funded

---

56   (NPR - When Did Companies Become People? 2014)

like 401K that are invested in the stock market. Yet that would drive up the stock market with more demand. Similarly, there are vast buyback of stocks that increase the stock price while also boosting executive bonus compensations.

Shareholders and the Executive Class

As Americans individually and through 401k programs own more stock in corporations, the ability of shareholders to participate in corporate issues is diffused among more people and in some cases among millions of people. Thus, the corporate managers are not beholden to the shareholders except for the value of the stock and payout of dividends. The various boards of directors became a power unto themselves voting for the best interests of the directors and to maintain the loyalty of the senior managers. Loyalty of the dwindling number of managers and senior managers focuses more towards the board of directors. Loyalty becomes paramount. So, for those who have ambition for power, money, and status they focus upon concern for those higher up and by the way a job well done, while hoping and planning for the next promotion. Concern for the people, the corporation, and various communities is of little concern. The boards of directors use profits to bolster or raise stock prices through stock buybacks, which weakens the long-term health of the corporation and stock dividends.

However, a fully functioning capitalistic system not dominated by a few companies, will force the corporations to be more efficient with financial, physical, and human resources. The less the competition and the more the intertwining of corporations with government, the less efficient the process becomes and the more profitable for a few key individuals.

Corporations naturally seek ways to improve the profitability. One way started under President Ronald Reagan by beginning in 1981 to eliminate the New Deal.

Chapter 4

The New Deal

The Great Depression (1929-1939) was the largest economic downturn in the US and the world. The lowest point was in 1933 with half the banks failing, lifetime savings being lost, mortgages foreclosed on, and fifteen million people unemployed (20%). President Herbert Hoover (Republican) believed that the government was not a job creator nor sustainer. That the economy on its own would recover.

Within one hundred days of being in office in 1933, President Franklin D. Roosevelt (FDR) created several key agencies that dramatically affected the US and future generations by creating a strong social safety net:[57]

- Federal Deposit Insurance Corporation – protected depositors accounts
- Security and Exchange Commission - regulated the stock market and prevent abuse
- Works Progress Administration – created 8.5 million jobs
- Tennessee Valley Authority – controlled flooding and created electric power for rural America
- Social Security Act – created unemployment, disability, and pension benefits
- Fair Labor and Standards Act (1938) – established minimum wages, overtime pay, and child labor standards for full an part-time workers in both private sector and the federal, state, and local governments.[58]

---

57   (History - Great Depression History n.d.)

58   (US Department of Labor - Handy Reference Guide to the Fair Labor Standards Act 2016)

Creation of a Vast Middle Class

Prior to New Deal, the elderly would move into the small homes of their children, often having a bed in a dining room, a hallway, or sharing with one of their grandchildren of even the opposite sex, while having little to no medical, dental, nor eye care.

With the New Deal, the elderly gradually would no longer be in poverty during unemployment, disability, nor retirement. Coupled with the productive corporations, together they created a vast middle class. Middle class elderly people were able to live out their lives in retirement communities, assisted care facilities, and finally nursing homes.

However, then and to this day, strong forces do not agree that US government should provide a social safety net. Instead they believe in extremely limited government and independent free markets. They believe that the New Deal created and continues to create people dependent upon the government, reduces liberty and prosperity. That without the burdensome agencies like those just listed and many others, the US would be richer, stronger, more self-sufficient, and continue to create a nation of liberty and not of lazy dependents upon the government, productive people, and the job creators. For ninety years those forces have worked and continue now more energetically in a variety of ways to dismantle the New Deal openly and quietly.

For example, a variety of forecasts say that Social Security taxes will have zero reserves by 2033[59] and the total revenue will be 100% of the total payout until at least 2040. However, Congress can make minor adjustments that help the program. They include raising the maximum income that can be taxed to be no greater than $135,000, legalize more immigrants so that they too pay into Social Security (though many say that they do and won't be able to collect), adjust the age upwards to begin collecting Social Security, and several other actions. The only one agreed to, is to raise the age. The other issue

59   (David Pattison -Social Security Office of Retirment and Disability - Social Security Trust Fund Cash Flows and Reserves 2015)

is Congress uses the Reserve fund built up over seventy years for programs that the total Federal Budget does not cover. Then saying that the Federal government owes the Social Security Trust Fund the borrowed money.

There are suggestions to convert Social Security to stock market purchases and/or allow insurance companies to manage Social Security portfolios. Thus, the government would not be in the business of transfer payments. Instead, companies would collect what were taxes, call them investments, and insurance companies or stock companies would then manage the retirement accounts. Notice how the wording changed in what was just written. This writing started with "benefit" and switched to "taxes".

Those Republicans that are against Social Security view it as a benefit that neither businesses nor the government should be involved with. Instead they call it a tax. And taxes are just part of the income stream to the government. The government has deficits that must be paid and in the past people thought that Social Security was specifically for them. That was and is a misunderstanding. Instead the language is quietly changing to call it a tax which means the government can change how the funds can be used. In any case, the reality is that for decades the government has dipped into the Social Security Trust Fund to "better use the idle funds" for the benefit of America.

A current example is with the COV19 economic impact. Individuals and corporations both pay 6.2% for a total of 12.4% of an individual's pay up to a maximum of $135,000 per year. Corporations will delay paying individual and corporate shares of the Social Security tax (note the word tax again) until December 31, 2020 to the IRS. The companies will continue to withhold funds from individuals. Thus, the companies temporarily hold on to the 12.4% of the Social Security payments until the end of 2020. Then the companies are to pay what was withheld.[60] Forces that want to dismantle Social Security love this because on the one hand that immediately boosts cash to struggling companies and the economy; while on the other hand, it hurts the financial

60   (Sarah O'Brien - CNBC - Companies get to defer payroll tax payments 2020)

viability of Social Security. Those that are in favor of Social Security fear that that this is a clever way to weaken Social Security and that the further legislation might be passed absolving the companies of paying back the 12.4% that was not paid to the IRS.

At the heart of the tension in the US over the social safety net programs is the conflict between individualism versus community, socialism versus capitalism, and minimal versus mama-government.

The Great Tension – Appropriate Size Government

The idea and deep feeling of freedom is in the very air and culture of America. Yet, there is a tension. A fundamental tension in American society is "I versus We". Many Americans love liberty. They proudly display flags, license plates, stickers, hats, tee-shirts, sweatshirts, placards, in daily life, political campaigns, and as with the slogans such as:

- Live Free or Die
- Liberty or Death
- Religious Freedom
- First Amendment rights (freedom of speech)
- Second Amendment rights (freedom to carry guns)
- States' Rights
- Born to be free
- The Stars and Stripes of the American Flag Forever
- I believe in the Constitution
- Constitutional Rights!

Radio, television, newspapers, magazines, universities, seminaries, and politicians also use these items and slogans showing that they are true patriots and lovers of Freedom. Yet, there is a tension.

Some believe deep within their core being that freedom is first and foremost focused upon oneself and the US. Upon "I". That the only responsibility people have to others is to guarantee freedom to others, so long as it coincides with their religious beliefs. They are willing to fight, to be armed, and to die to protect those freedoms.

On the other hand, many Americans believe that freedom means that people are individuals and are part of a community. That they have a responsibility to themselves and to the general welfare of the larger community. Democrats will argue that the Preamble to the US Constitution states, "In order to promote the general welfare." Their interpretation is that embedded in the Constitution, the Federal Government has the duty to be concerned about "issues such as poverty, housing, food and other economic and social welfare issues facing the citizenry which were of central concern to the framers". Republicans on the other hand argue that the Amendments to the Constitution and other sections limits the Federal Government's role and that it is up to the States to determine what if any social safety net there will be.[61]

Thus, while in the past ninety years, trying to overtly undo the American social safety net particularly Social Security, which is really undoing the New Deal and subsequent programs, is the "Third Rail of American politics." That is an analogy to electric trains. The rail that carries the electric power is called "the third rail." So, to touch that rail is a guarantee of death. Consequently, politicians have stayed away from directly weakening the Social Security particularly and the other New Deal type programs. Nevertheless, in the past Republicans have been quietly changing he programs to free people from the enfeebling mama state and help make corporations more competitive internationally. Now, they are more willing to a more openly address these issues.

To get the needed support, Republicans overtly appeal to God.

---

61   (Martha F. Davis - American Constitution Society - To Promote the General Welfare 2011)

Chapter 5

God

Religion was involved from the 1500's to today in the creation of the modern-day United States of America. Being at times like a quiet ocean then overflowing with massive waves surfers love. This chapter summarizes those religious political drives.

1500's to the Early 1800's

While the international race between England, France, Spain, and Holland was for land, wealth, and power, clerics also came to civilize the natives and supply religious services to their own people. Each wave of immigration brought the religion of their homeland. The Irish, Italians, French, and Spanish brought Catholicism. The Germans brought Lutheranism and Catholicism. The Dutch the Reformed Church. The English the Anglican Church. While the slaves brought their African religions, clerics of their masters converted them to Christianity. The clerics attempted to convert the Native Americans. Then there were religious refugees such as the Pilgrims, Mennonites, Hutterites, and others. The first religious colleges were Harvard, Yale, Princeton, and several other institutions formed to supply ministers and to educate the elite young men.

The early immigrants spread out from Maine to Florida to the Mississippi River Valley taking their various religions with them. For the most part, with a few exceptions, people were free to worship as they pleased. Though the Europeans brought their biases and prejudices with them that continue to play out into the Twenty-first Century.

Thomas Jefferson, the principal author of the Declaration of Independence in 1776 and President of the US from 1801-1809, wrote Jefferson Bible. Using scissors, he extracted from the Bible only the sayings of Jesus. In his edited words:

> In extracting the pure principles which he (Jesus) taught, we should ... strip off the artificial vestments in which they have been muffled by priests, who have travestied them into various forms, as instruments of riches and power to themselves. We must dismiss ... their essences ... their logos, ... and daemons ... of nonsense. We must reduce ... to the simple ... very words only of Jesus, (eliminating ambiguities which followers did not understand) ...There will be found remaining the most sublime and benevolent code of morals which has ever been offered to man. I have performed this operation for my own use, by cutting verse by verse out of the printed book, and arranging the matter which is evidently his, and which is as easily distinguishable as diamonds in a dunghill. The result is ... pure and unsophisticated doctrines.[62]

There is a fundamental highly political misunderstanding of role of religion in the creation of the Declaration of Independence and the US Constitution. Evangelical and/or "traditional" Protestants have claimed that Christianity was central to the early history of the United States and that the nation was founded on Judeo-Christian principles. They point to the use of prayer in Congress, national days of prayer and thanksgiving and the invocation of God as the source of our "unalienable rights" in the Declaration of Independence. [63]

Secularists respond that many of the founding fathers were deists (believe in a general concept of God) and that they created the two key documents on secular foundations. They further cite the utter absence of biblical references in our principal founding documents and note that the God of the Declaration of Independence is not described in a scriptural idiom as "God the

---

62   (Wikipedia - Jefferson Bible 2020)

63   (Seidel, Andrew L. - The Founding Myth 2019)

Father" but instead in deistic terms as a "Creator" and "supreme judge of the world."

Although both sides have some evidence, neither is persuasive. Ultimately however, the role of deism in the American founding is just too complex to force into such simplistic formulas.[64]

> ... those men who signed the Declaration of Independence, sat in the Confederation Congress, or participated in the Constitutional Convention for whom we have reliable information, the vast bulk were fairly traditional in the religious lives. The presumed deists comprise a fairly small group, although most are prominent "A list" founders like Thomas Jefferson, George Washington, George Mason, James Madison, John Adams, Alexander Hamilton, and Benjamin Franklin.

> Many of the founders were Freemasons who encountered considerable opposition from organized religion, especially from the Roman Catholic Church, and from various states. Freemasonry teaches morality, charity, and obedience to the law of the land. For admission the applicant is required to be an adult male believing in the existence of a Supreme Being and in the immortality of the soul. ... Generally, Freemasonry in Latin countries has attracted freethinkers and anticlericals, whereas in the Anglo-Saxon countries, the membership is drawn largely from among white Protestants.[65]

In general, the Founding Fathers of the US understood the religious wars in Europe. They purposefully founded the Constitution based on tolerance of religion and to keep a separation of church and state. They were interested in avoiding the divisiveness of religious conflict and even possibly of religion as a political weapon which it now is in the early Twenty-first Century.

Nevertheless, religion did eventually have a significant impact upon the

---

64   (Staloff 2020)

65   (Staloff 2020)

growing country. While many immigrants came to the US for economic reasons and political freedom, there were groups, such as the Mennonites, Hutterites, Pilgrims, and other groups, that came specifically for religious freedom. Additionally, many other immigrants brought their religion with them such as the Lutherans, Catholics, Anglicans, etc. They formed churches, schools, universities, and social agencies.

Revivals

The several Great Rivals show that many immigrants were not churched. The aim was preaching plain gospel truths which "...were God's absolute sovereignty, man's total depravity, and Christi's atoning love." [66] These rivals increased and decreased like ocean waves at a beach during the 1800's and through the 1900's. Billy Graham revivals is one of the most famous. People fervently turned to God and then in time many fell away. Only to have another revival. Politicians who might or might not have been true believers used the followers to gain political influence and in turn businesses also used the followers to gain political power to further business friendly legislation.

In some areas of the US there were so many revivals that some people quipped that the area was "burned over" meaning that there weren't many people left to convert. One such area in upstate New York was where Joseph Smith founded Mormonism.

Religious leaders in the South also converted slaves to Christianity. Part of the impetus was to save souls. It was also a means to convince the slaves to be docile and accept their God ordained position as slaves.

Biblical Literalism

In the late 1800's Biblical literalism started to become widespread. Eventually, thirty percent of the US believes that the Bible is literal, inerrant, and the Word of God. Literalism states that the average person can understand the

---

66   (Ahlstrom 1975) page 417.

Bible just as the authors wrote it. That it says what it says and means what it says, unless there is a sign that it is allegory, poetry, or some other meaning.

Therefore, the stories in Genesis such as the Creation, Noah's Ark, and the long lives in the genealogies, etc. are factually correct.[67] Many seminaries and preachers teach that the Holy Spirit guided the very fingers of the original authors of the Bible to write every stroke and mark. Any doubts about that are because of a regenerate mind that refuses to believe the truth.

That the Scriptures are sealed to such a person. "The Bible is incomprehensible to those who are lacking in the inward personal adjustment to God, which alone insures a spiritual understanding." [68] Further there is no sense in wasting time arguing with such people for they will never believe. That rationalism that has crept into Biblical teaching which leads to ridicule and rejection of sound doctrine is based on ignorance[69] – willful and deceitful ignorance.[70]

To understand the American Mind, it is important to understand the three previous paragraphs. That Biblical literalism is potent force in the United States of America. That many laypeople, ministers, Congressmen, Senators, military leaders, commentators, and some Presidents firmly or at least vaguely believe or accept Biblical literalism.

As you read the following sections and chapters keep remember this view. It will help you understand how it influenced and influences American politics on school boards, local, State, and Federal elections, and increasingly in rulings by judges at various levels. This will be shown in the following sections.

---

67   (Wikipedia - Biblical Literalism 2020)

68   (Chafer 1947 Eleventh Edition 1973) Vol 1, page 9.

69   (Chafer 1947 Eleventh Edition 1973) Vol 1, page viii.

70   (Chafer 1947 Eleventh Edition 1973) Vol 1, page 118.

Prohibition of Alcohol

The influence of Christian conservative churches in the US is clearly visible with the implementation of the prohibition of the production, distribution, and sale of alcohol. The movement became a powerful national force when the Women's Christian Temperance Union and the Anti-Saloon League (three of the six leaders were Christian ministers[71]) joined forces. They believed that alcohol consumption destroyed lives, was immoral and degraded society. Capitalizing on the fervor of World War I that supported "the boys at war" they gained support for the Prohibition.[72] By 1919, 45 of 48 States ratified the 18th Amendment to the Constitution prohibiting the production, distribution, and sale of alcohol. Interestingly it was legal for people to consume alcohol.[73]

However, as the States passed laws the full force of the implementation became clearer, many people became disenchanted with Prohibition. The mafia and other illegal operations became substantially powerful. Franklin D. Roosevelt included in his November 1932 platform for President of the US to end Prohibition. As one of his first acts was the very rapid passage by December 1933 of the 21st Amendment to the Constitution of the US that repealed Prohibition.[74]

Anti-Evolution

At the same time, another Christian force became politically powerful. In 1925, the State of Tennessee passed a law prohibiting the teaching of evolution. For violating that law, John Scopes, a high school teacher, was arrested. William Jennings Bryant, three times a US Presidential Candidate, and staunch anti-evolutionist acted as the prosecutor. Clarence Darrow's goal as defense attorney "…was to debunk fundamentalist Christianity and raise awareness of a narrow, fundamentalist interpretation of the Bible." The very

71   (Westerville Public Library - Anti-Saloon League Museum n.d.)

72   (History.com Editors - 18th and 21st Amendments 2020)

73   (Wikipedia - Eighteenth Amendment to the United States Constitution 2020)

74   (History.com Editors - 18th and 21st Amendments 2020)

publicized trial became a national sensation in newspapers and on the radio. In nine minutes of deliberation, the jury found Scopes guilty and was fined $100[75] which is about $1,500 in 2020.[76] Clarence Darrow paid the fine.

Also, in 1925, the States of Mississippi and Texas passed similar anti-evolution legislation. While efforts in other States did not pass, the strong anti-evolution stance remains a force in US education into the 21st Century. Anti-evolutionism has morphed into Intelligent Design[77] which states "...certain features of the universe and of living things are best explained by an intelligent cause, not an undirected process such as natural selection."[78]

Because of vocal political backlash, 60% of science and biology teachers either don't teach evolution or "teach evolution, but not so you'd notice…. This 60% "qualify" their teaching, going through the "teach the controversy" line of thinking, apologize for teaching evolution, or limit the subject to microbes. In other words, despite evolution winning court cases, it is losing in the classrooms.[79]

The anti-evolutions clearly state that Darwinism leads to immorality, evil, homosexuality, and the destruction of human civilization. For example, "Darwinism justified and encouraged the Nazi views on both race and war. If the Nazi party had fully embraced and consistently acted on the belief that all humans were descendants of Adam and Eve and equal before the creator God, as taught in both the Old Testament and New Testament Scriptures, the holocaust would never have occurred." [80] Furthermore, "Expunging

75   (History.com Editors - Scopes Trial 2019)

76   (Dollar Times - Calculate the Value of dollars in today's times 2020)

77   (History.com Editors - Scopes Trial 2019)

78   (Intelligent Design - What is Intelligent Design? n.d.)

79   (Paul Fidalgo - Center for Inquiry - Eugenie Scott and Bertha Vazquez on "Reaching the 60%" for Evolution Education 2016)

80   (Jerry Bergman - Answers In Genesis - Darwinism and the Nazi Race Holocaust 1999)

the Judeo-Christian doctrine of the divine origin of humans from mainline German (liberal) theology and its schools, and replacing it with Darwinism, openly contributed to the acceptance of Social Darwinism that culminated in the tragedy of the holocaust." Therefore, the teaching of evolution is *evil*.

These views contributed to the growth of homeschooling, conservative religious elementary and high schools, as well as universities such as Liberty University, Hillsdale College, Praeger University, Dallas Theological Seminary, Trinity Evangelical Seminary, and many others.

Christian Conservative position for the Republican Party [81]

Pat Buchanan, a political strategist and former US Presidential candidate, outlined the Christian Conservative position for the Republican Party. He said that in most elections thirty percent of the eligible voters turn out – and that is in a good year. So, all that is needed to win is 16% of the vote. Elections are close. So, all that is needed to win is 1% or a few percent of the vote. Christian Conservatives can deliver that one to a few percent to help the Republican Party win. Forget the liberal states on the East and West Coasts like California, New York, and the rest. Instead concentrate on the vast interior of the US. Here there are many Christian Churches. We will work with them on the issues that are important to them. Issues like abortion, homosexuality, anti-evolution, etc. Once we make our power known, the Republican Party will have to do what we tell them.

That way, we will control the State Legislatures and Governorships. We will control the Senate which approves members of the President's Cabinet, Supreme Court Judges, and the vast number of Federal Judges, and other federal appointees. They will all then be friendly to Christian values.

---

81   I am not sure who it was and when it happened. Perhaps it was Pat Robertson or perhaps Pat Buchanan in a TV interview in the late 1970's to the 1980's. What I do remember clearly is what the person said.

As we gain control, we will then change the laws in the school boards, counties, states, and federal levels to be Christian friendly. So, even if the liberals could win back the States and the Federal governments, they will have to argue and fight through all fifty States and both Houses of Congress. Even then, if they were to do that, the courts will have lifetime conservative judges who are friendly to the Christian Conservative values.

It will take fifty years for liberals to get back where they are now. By then we should be able to re-surge and push them back.

Currently, a strong element of the US political leadership is Conservative Christians. They are successfully integrating those beliefs into the political will and the American Mind. While many presidents have been religious to various degrees, only George Bush Jr and Donald Trump have vigorously openly supported Conservative Christianity. As a result, their religious views have significantly influenced the selection of Cabinet members, lifetime appointees to federal judgeships such as the Supreme Court of the US, Ambassadors, and State governments. In turn that influences several key features internal and foreign policy.

Armageddon

Christian Conservatives believe that there will be a great battle between good and evil anti-Christ before The Day of Judgment south of Haifa in Israel. Some believe that the Ant-Christ is the UN, European Union, Russia, or China. Regardless, they believe that the Book of Revelation, the last book in the Christian Bible, is an accurate forecast and so it quietly drives their foreign policy. Of particular interest is helping Israel regain its former Biblical boundaries.

Evil and Love

They believe that humans are by their very nature sinful and evil. That the world is corrupt and only by salvation through Jesus Christ will mankind be saved, which will happen in the next life. That there is a great war going on for the very soul of the United States, which is a beacon of hope for the world. That liberalism has corrupted the United States by pushing homosexuality, evolution, abortion, and abandoning the fundamental Judaeo-Christian principles that created the US and are embedded in the US Declaration of Independence and the US Constitution. Thus, liberals and liberalism are considered *evil*. An *evil* that must be fought. As vocal as the Conservatives are on this fundamental issue, liberals continue to sleep, dream, and ignore the basic nature of the war waged against them.

The Prosperity Gospel

There is a strong element in Conservative Christianity that God wants people to be prosperous. That through belief in Jesus, hard work, positive thinking, confession, and donations, believers will have wealth, health, happiness, and prosperity. Believers that are prosperous and happy are so because God has blessed them. Those that are not, have not embraced the Prosperity Gospel.

This view carries over into politics, government, and legislation. That it is the job of the government to protect its people against crime and enemies. But it is not the job of the government to take care of people. Rather, people will be happy, healthy, wealthy, and wise through the Prosperity Gospel. Thus, it is necessary to cut programs that enfeeble people and to get people to take care of themselves. So they work to eliminate welfare, Social Security, Medicare, Medicaid, and liberal education that teaches big government and socialism is good.

Sex

Conservative theology and politics states that sex is only in marriage between one man and one woman and that every pregnancy has a right life and abortion is evil. They want to amend the Constitution of the US and of each state to read, "Marriage is only between one man and one woman" and that "a human is formed at the moment of conception and has a right to life." That way, if liberals ever get back into power, they will have to work through making a change to the Constitution which is a very expensive and laborious process, as well as change the Constitution of each of the fifty states.

Such actions include prohibitions to all forms of contraception such as prophylaxis, any form of reading materials, abortion pills, abortions, and assisting people by any means to have an abortion.

Furthermore, schools will only teach abstinence only, homosexuality is against nature and God, and that marriage is only between one man and one woman. Schools that teach other views will lose funding and teachers will lose their licenses and jobs.

Home schooling

Because Conservatives feel that liberalism is an Evil, an Evil that must be fought, they want their children to learn only what is Godly an learn the true Judeo-Christian principles that created the US. To have every day in school, prayer, Bible reading, and the Pledge of Allegiance to the Flag of the United States. To learn that Creationism and not evolution is true. In schools to have strong morals and more discipline. To have Bible study in every school level and know that the Bible is the foundation of morals for oneself and the US.

Because the public schools resist their proposed changes, they have formed strong home schooling programs, their own school systems, continue working to change public education to be more conservative, and transfer funds from the public education systems to the home schools and their private schools.

In the meantime, other conservative forces are working to,

Destroy public education

Many Conservative Christians and the Catholic hierarchy deeply want to either have public education be based upon Christian principles and their interpretation of history. Until 1962, each school day started with the Pledge of Allegiance to the Flag of the United States of America; a reading from the

Bible; and, then a prayer. Then the Supreme Court abolished prayer in public schools. That caused an outrage in the conservative communities. They felt that public education would become immoral. That children would not learn about faith in God, the creator of all good, and the basis for the formation of the United States. That the country would eventually lose its place as the leader of the free world. That this was a communist plot to destroy America.

So, conservative Christians along with the Catholic Church campaigned to get public funds to support their educations systems to include homeschooling. However, in the US, funding of public education is a mixture of federal, state, and local initiatives. Frequently people without children and conservative Christians will not vote to support funding of public education. Yet they want money from that system to support their system. Additionally, public schools are mandated to supply transportation to non-secular schools. Increasingly, there are movements demanding that the state pay for science, math, history, and other non-religious subjects in their schools. Which then includes paying for the part of the buildings and grounds used for secular activities such as sports, parking, building maintenance, and teacher pay. All these efforts siphon money from the public education system. If local governments do not turn funds over to religious schools, some conservatives threaten to inundate the public schools with their children, which would result in overcrowding, insufficient resources, and political turmoil.

As a result, over the decades Republican State Houses have reduced funding to public universities. These efforts have made many such universities expensive for the average American student. Many of them graduate from college with $26,900 for graduates of public four-year schools and $32,600 for graduates of private nonprofit four-year schools.[82] These students whether they graduate or not must repay the loans with interest. In many cases students have much more debt and of course less debt for those with the sufficient family financial support.

---

82   (Hess 2019)

The result is that many students are more concerned with getting the classes completed while working to get the necessary income than mastering the course materials. Classes then instead of growing minds become just a 'ticket to punch' to get a good paying job. However, there are so many college graduates that the college diploma is no longer a guarantee of a good paying job. Rather a college degree is now what the high school diploma was in the 1960's and earlier.

Project Blitz

Project Blitz's purpose is to enshrine a very particular vision of Christianity in county, State, and Federal laws and organizations throughout the United States. It seeks to "protect the free exercise of traditional Judeo-Christian religious values and beliefs in the public square, and to reclaim and properly define the narrative which supports such beliefs" and to have laws eliminate interference of Christian practice in the public square to include public schools and institutions such as the judiciary, legislatures, police, and media; supports conservative legislators at the local, state and federal level with public relations and messaging; and otherwise seeks to alter longstanding narratives of religious liberty issues. It encourages Bible readings and study in public schools and religious exemptions to LGBTQ civil rights protections and women's reproductive healthcare.

The Project has model legislation, proclamations, and talking points for state and local legislators who wish to introduce bills that support religious freedom and liberty. Additionally, there are models and strategies for gender and sexuality, biblical literacy in public schools, recognition of Christian heritage and Christmas Day, and displays of the national motto. It also provides talking points.

While there have been many organizations campaigning against Project Blitz, it has had a subtle yet significant impact upon the American legal structure and continues to do so. In 2019, after much outrage by the left, the organization changed its' name and has gone underground.

Current estimates are that it includes at least 950 legislators at the federal and state levels. The legislators that support Project Blitz are not public.[83]

There are three tiers to the Project:

> Tier 1. Simple safe actions that gently move the public to the deeper structural changes. The simple ones are to have "In God We Trust," which is the national motto, placed in all public building, schools, and equipment. Many court room and legislative chambers have the motto prominently displayed. It is common to see police cars and fire engines with the motto discretely yet prominently displayed. Some vehicle license plates display the motto. Many people do not pay attention to these subtle changes. However, conservative Christians consider such displays as their continuing growing influence on establishing that the US is based upon their version of God and that they are saving the US from moral destruction. Meanwhile Conservative Christians notice these subtle changes and feel their political power growing.

> Tier 2. Pass resolutions that proclaim the conservative Christian views. For instance, that the US was founded upon Judeo-Christian principles, marriage is between one man and one woman, that religious people do not have to do anything that violates their conscience or religion, that companies have religious freedom to not do activities that violate the owners' conscience or religion, that religions have freedoms that shall not be trampled upon, the Bible is the official book of the US, etc.

> Tier 3. Pass legislation and amend the constitutions of the states and the federal government for the resolutions in Tier 2.[84]

---

83   (Frederick Clarkson - Project Blitz by Any Other Name 2019)

84   (David Taylor - The Guardian - Project Blitz: the legislative assault by Christian nationalists to reshape America 2018)

The basic view is, "If you are a more liberal Christian, a Jew, or a Muslim, or a non-believer of any sort, or whatever you happen to be, you're a second class citizen at best." [85]

Presidential decrees are a simple effective and politically powerful way to support Christian Conservatives. One example is exempting birth control mandates from insurance policies based upon deeply held religious beliefs of corporations. [86]

Creating a theocracy

The Conservative goal is to create the US as a theocracy where true Judeo-Christian conservative values and dogma are the law of the land from school boards, cities, counties, states, and to the federal government, and guided by their clerics. Thus, to have Christian conservationism deep into the blood and bones of every American.

Seems the same as Muslims want or have in Iran, Saudi Arabia, Indonesia, Pakistan, and other Muslim countries that Conservative Christians rage against. Meanwhile liberal Christians and their clerics continuing dreaming of the past, present, and future not understanding nor caring that their churches, liberal legislation and government, and cherished freedoms that are taken for granted, are disappearing. They happily sleep and congratulate themselves about making ineffective plans to resurrect their churches, schools, universities, laws, and politics.

Meanwhile their country changes.

---

85   (David Taylor - The Guardian - Project Blitz: the legislative assault by Christian nationalists to reshape America 2018)

86   (Daley 2020) Roberts, Liberal Justices Wary of Trump Exemptions to Birth Control Mandate.

Chapter 6

Country

Americans tend to have two distinct views of the United States. The Conservatives take deep emotional pride in how the US was formed upon Judeo-Christian values. That Jesus was present at the creation and signing of the Declaration of Independence and the formation of the US Constitution. That God's quiet influence was evident in the Manifest Destiny in the creation of the Thirteen Colonies, winning the land from the Allegheny Mountains to the Mississippi River from the French. Buying the Northwest Territories from the Napoleon. Gaining what is now the Southwestern US from the Spanish in 1848. The purchasing what is now Alaska from Russia in 1867. Annexing Hawaii in 1898 to prevent foreign powers from acquiring it. Spain ceding Puerto Rico to the US after the 1898 Spanish American War. That God's hand was creating a land of freedom and opportunity.

Thus, the Conservatives see God's guidance in American actions when the country follows Gods' laws and influence. The US was a beacon on the hill to the world – particularly the Christian world.

On the other hand, a significant number of Americans believe that the US was founded upon secular views of freedom. That while the US territorial gains listed above are factual, the interpretation is not. Rather, the interpretation is the US took the opportunities for expansion. That there was a destiny to create a new land of freedom and opportunity. However, there were significant human rights issues in the process. As previously stated, 400,000 slaves were brought to the US. Millions of Native Americans were killed, their lands stolen, and the remaining tribes pushed onto confined reservations with supposedly the rights of independent nations. Millions of immigrants came to the US to labor in the factories, farms, and sweatshops. Eventually a vibrant middle arose.

Those are two distinct views that Americans have of themselves.

Into this come several more views.

The Greatest Generation

At the end of WWII many Germans, Japanese, and Italians accepted that they lost the war and the Americans, British, Canadians, Australians, New Zealanders, Russians, and others had won. The Germans, Japanese, and Italians then went to work. They industriously remade their cities, factories, education, social systems, and went on with their lives. They created a mindset that focused on creating a bright future.

On the other hand, Americans nostalgically look back to the Japanese attack on December 7, 1941 upon Pearl Harbor. That they were able to create an Army, Air Force, and Navy to fight both Germany and Japan. Without the American "Arsenal of Democracy" supplying weapons, ammunition, ships, trucks, tanks, planes, and soldiers, the British, Canadians, and many other allies along with the Russians probably would not have won WWII. Thus, Americans look back at WWII with the nostalgia that glorifies their ancestral efforts, contributions, and sacrifices that led to victory. Many movies and books create the justified sense of victory which in turn many Americans have pride of what their ancestors did and then came home to create an economic miracle. They created a vast new middle class who would have creature comforts and educational systems virtually unheard of in civilization. Thus, that generation became known as "The Greatest Generation."

However, in contrast to the Germans, Japanese, and Italians at the end of World War II, many Americans now contentedly view themselves as part of that "Greatest Generation." As a group they are dimly aware that the rest of the world has been assiduously working to create more wealth for themselves and in several cases creating more wealth per capita than what America now does.

That dim sense of creeping loss slips into the American psyche which naturally gravitates to the positiveness of those that will Make America Great Again. That there is no other country like the US which has created massive wealth for its people. "We did it before. We can do it again."

Inspired the world with freedom, but now...

At the core of American feelings is that they inspire the world with freedom and opportunity. That the rest of the world desires to be like them. Which is why millions of people have come, and still want to come, to the US.

After World War I, the US retired from the world stage contented to be inward focused and follow George Washington's advice to steer clear of permanent alliances with any foreign nation.[87]

That sense of isolationism is a core feeling in the US. Especially since America is bounded by on the East and West Coasts by two oceans; to the North by a friendly quiet country; to the South that many Americans perceive as invaders taking away jobs and what the US stands for. So, While Woodrow Wilson helped create the League of Nations, the US opted inward and refused to join. Some feel the Wilson fatigued himself so much with the fight that he became so ill that he effectively was not the President for the rest of time in office.

Franklin Roosevelt realized the world threat from both Germany and the Japan in the 1930's. Through various means he supplied support to the British. It was not until the attack on Pearl Harbor that the US entered upon the world stage as a military and political power.

It led in creating various organizations such as North Atlantic Treaty Organization, South East Asia Treaty Organization, the Marshall Plan to resurrect Europe, International Monetary System, General Agreement on Tariffs and Trade, and many other international actions.

---

87   (Sarah Pruitt - George Washington Warned Against Political Infighting in His Farewell Address 2020)

From the beginning of World War Two the US until around 2016 led the Free World. Since then it has been retreating into a self-interested country caring only for its' own affairs.

Nevertheless, large segments of the US fervently believe in the greatness of the US. They take pride in waving the Stars and Stripes, chanting "USA. USA. USA." In having a military force that is about 45% of the entire world's military budgets and 15% of the US Budget.[88] Yet, one American Lieutenant General said, "Obesity is a national security issue." [89] Which reflects upon the entire military and the American society. It has the highest medical costs per capita with the one of the lowest health outcomes.[90] Similarly, the US education system ranks among the lowest of the developed nations with fierce efforts to total dismantle or destroy the public education system.[91] The US is ceding strength in trade, technology, skills, and institutions.[92]

Meanwhile liberals are aware of these issues; yet, they are ineffective in addressing any of them. The result is that the US is turning away from addressing fundamental issues, giving up its world leadership, and happily embrace the views of the ...

Conservative Political Action Conference (CPAC)

The Conservative Political Action Conference (CPAC) "is the largest and most influential gathering of conservatives in the world. Launched in 1974, CPAC brings together once a year hundreds of conservative organizations, thousands of activists, millions of viewers and the best and brightest leaders

---

88   (Peter G. Peterson Foundation - U.S. Defense Spending Compared to Other Countries 2020)

89   (Mark Hertling, Lieutant General - Obesity is a National Security Issue 2012)

90   (Peter G. Peterson Foundation - How Does the U.S. Healthcare System Compare to Other Countries? 2019)

91   See Chapter 5, God, Destroy Public Education

92   (Antony J. Blinken and Robert Kagan - Brookings - 'America First' is only making the world worse. Here's a better approach. 2019)

in the world. Over 19,000 people attended CPAC 2019… with 60% of attendees experiencing the conference for the first time, half of whom are college aged and younger."[93]

Key concerns are the fight against socialism, pro right to life (anti-abortion), and the fight against Obama's coup against President Trump.[94]

The 2020 Conference's Agenda items included:[95]

The Fate of Our Culture and Nation Hangs in the Balance

- The Coup on The Republic
- The Left's Takeover of Our Culture
- Threats to the Electoral College
- Opposing the National Popular Vote Scheme
- Protecting the Ballot Box & Defeating The Left's Voter Fraud Machine
- How the Left Justifies Acts of Violence
- Protecting the Second Amendment (Gun Rights)
- Freedom of Speech in America… And How We are Losing It
- The Courts Are Rigged
- Weaponize Social Media
- Without Religious Freedom, What's Left?
- Big Media's Efforts to Shut Down Conservative Speech Online
- Socialism: Wrecker of Nations and Destroyer of Societies
- Stopping Socialism: Exposing and Defeating the Socialist Plot to Hijack America
- Prescription for Failure: The Ills of Socialized Medicine
- Disaster of Free College
- Double Down on Tax Cuts

---

93   (Conservative Political Action Conference 2020)

94   (Conservative Political Action Conference 2020)

95   (Conservativ Political Action Conference - Agenda 2020)

- The Future of the Family
- Celebrate Adoption!
- Help Others Recognize the Left's Powerful Propaganda Tactic

The Global Struggle for Resources and the
21st Century *Socialist Axis of Evil*

- What's Really Happening on Our Southern Border
- E Pluribus... Out of Many, What?
- Rewarding Lawbreakers: Sanctuary Cities & Porous Borders
- Israel: What Should the Map Look Like?
- Be Pro-Israel
- Defeating the Climate Delusion
- A CO2 Climate Crisis?

Among the many conservative groups that support the CPAC agenda yet not officially recognized by CPAC is…

White Nationalism

From the 1970's to the 2020's many American's felt that liberals have attacked their religion, the right to own guns, impinged on their free speech, reduced their economic wellbeing, outsourced their jobs, given in to the New World Order, are destroying the American economy with fears of Global Climate Change hoax, given more to the lazy than justified, seen their purchasing power significantly diminish, and the white population decreasing from 90% in 1950 to under 50% by 2050. So, many turned to White Nationalism as the way to improve their position and go back to when American was great – also might be known as "Make America Great Again."

The unofficial National motto was from the time of the American Revolution till 1956 was "E pluribus unum". "Out of Many One". It appeared on the National Seal and currency. Then due to the Cold War with Russia and to emphasize that God was on the American side, the Motto was changed to "In

God We Trust" on both the National Seal and the currency.[96] One result of the subtle change was the US began to lose focus on integrating many diverse people that was a strength. It also quietly reinforced the underlying prejudice of many but not all whites against minorities such as African Americans, Hispanics, American Indians, and other foreigners. It was a symbolic change. Yet changing symbols have an effect.

White Nationalists tend to belong to ultra-Conservative churches which are fighting to save the soul of the US as they see it. They believe that Christ should be the ruler of the US. That the US should be for whites only. That Christian principles which includes being free to be left alone from most government are what created the great US nation. They passionately believe in a vigorous strong military and police force. That to protect oneself, one must own guns because the government can't be trusted to protect its' citizens from various forms of tyranny and emergencies. Many have a romantic view of US history as the self-made rugged individual man. A person that built his house, farmed his land, and was free to live and think as he pleased.

They rewrite the history and the myths of the US to align with their views and teach their children the true history, faith, and need for independence. Putting all this together is what is meant by American Exceptionalism. That the US is a great country because white people believed in Jesus and gave their lives to Him. That the country is falling apart because evil liberals are allowing foreigners to take their jobs, rights, and religion away.

Thus, they have a need for guns to protect those rights.

---

96   (Wikipedia - In God We Trust 2020)

Chapter 7

Guns

As described in Chapter 1, Freedom, settlers in the 1500-1800's hunted for food, created their own security from thieves, and battled with both other European nations and with Indians. If they didn't have guns, then they probably won't have survived. In those days, settlers probably considered guns as people today consider hammers, screwdrivers, a stove, cars and computers as tools. It is natural. The tools are just there. Similarly, millions of Americans consider guns a natural part of their lives. They are just there.

So, feelings run high in the US about owning or limiting guns. The divide is deep and arises usually when there is a shooting that reaches the mass media. After the furor dies down, the political interest on the issue moves on to other topics.

Millions of voters are single issue voters on guns. Their only concern is the gun issue. They will vote solely on a candidate's stand on gun ownership and use. So, they only vote Republican because Republicans will protect their rights to own guns. A few others only vote Democratic because they feel that Democrats will eventually solve the gun issue. Both Republicans and Democrats win and lose elections because of their focus on guns.

A powerful lobbying group in Washington, DC and State elections is the National Rifle Association (NRA). They spend millions of dollars to ensure that the right to own guns is not taken away and the 2nd Amendment (a right to own guns) is not weakened nor eliminated. They also advocate for gun safety and training.

Conservatives say, "Liberals want to take the guns away." "Give them an inch on gun rights and soon they will take more and more of our gun rights away." "Take away guns from law abiding citizens and only the criminals will have guns." "We must resist all their attempts at gun control; otherwise we won't have any guns."

Liberals say that they do not want to take guns away. Rather, they want to protect people with sensible gun control. Yet, the liberals present global solutions that do not solve the specific types of deaths from guns. For example, locking up guns, adding trigger locks, fingerprint devices, registering all guns, and adding more permits to own guns, do not prevent the largest two portions of gun deaths which are from suicide and most homicides.

These hardcore positions prevent an unbiased analysis of the issue. Plus, the statistics can be more than confusing. Here is a statistical view of the year 2017:

- 39,773 deaths from rifles and pistols
- 60% suicide (23, 854)
- 37% murder (14,542)
- 3 % other (accident, law enforcement, undetermined)(Roughly 400 each).[97]

The FBI defines four or more deaths in one incident as a mass murder. 383 people died in a mass murder in 2018.[98]

As with all statistics and efforts to improve them, the devil is in the details. While distasteful to some people, many others consider suicide as a right and one has freedom to choose. That people for a variety of reasons want to end their lives and should have the right to do so. Others believe that suicide is a cry for help. While others believe it is against God's will and a sin to kill oneself. Without going into these issues, suicide is a deeply personal issue which does have affects upon others.

What actions allow people to have their weapons and reduce suicide? Especially, when those that do use guns to kill themselves lack the resources to

97   (John Gramlich - Pew Research Center - What the data says about gun deaths in the U.S. 2019)

98   (John Gramlich - Pew Research Center - What the data says about gun deaths in the U.S. 2019)

turn their lives around, don't know how to ask for help, are beyond depression, and society does not have the desire to help 20,000 plus people a year who do kill themselves with guns.

The murder statistic lumps together rage killing of a family member or other person(s) in an argument, criminals killing each other, self-protection killing of a criminal, and mentally incompetent people killing someone, as well as other categories. The breakdown of this data is not clear nor consistent across the fifty states. It appears, again appears, that something like 60% of homicides are involved with some sort of criminal activity using guns. So, if a criminal uses a gun there is a high probability that someone will be hurt or killed.

Numerous groups, such as The American Psychological Association have detailed a number of approaches to reducing the gun deaths.[99] However, due to the entrenched politics, religious views, and views about freedom, lack of funding, medical confidentiality, and possible lawsuits, reaching any viable means to reduce gun violence remains elusive in the US.

Europeans and other countries do not understand American love of guns. However, they do understand Americans who dislike guns.

Both the love and hate of guns are part of the American DNA and American political intrigue...

---

99   (American Psychological Association - Gun Violence: Prediction, Prevention, and Policy 2013)

Chapter 8

Political Intrigue

Republicans believe that politics is a rough contact sport. Therefore, since they are fighting for the soul of the US, anyone that disagrees with them is the enemy and since it is a war, anything goes to win. Though they will deny this while winking and blaming the opposition for all the ills in the US. On the other hand, Democrats dream on winning because the numbers are on their side and they believe that they have the best interests of the US. As a result, civil discourse and statesmen have disappeared from the US.

This chapter outlines the basic political intrigue in voting, Political Action Committees, Russia & China interference, religion, public retirement funds, and global climate change.

Voting

Some of the political intrigues with voting are related to the balance of power, the Electoral College, two Houses of Congress, Supreme Court, gerrymandering, voter suppression, and voter turnout.

Voting — Balance of Power

It is difficult for a non-American to understand the US national voting system. Originally it was setup to balance the power between large and small States. The fear was that if the voting was based solely upon the total popular vote, then presidential candidates would focus only on the large states and not pay attention to the small states, and the large states would have more influence on legislation than the small states. So, a system was needed to balance the powers between the large and small states. Thus, the Constitutional Convention in 1789 created the Electoral College, Two Houses of Congress, and the Supreme Court.

Voting — President and the Electoral College

For President, the Constitutional Convention created the Electoral College. It meets once every four years. Each Congressman and Senator has one vote. There are 435 Congressmen and 100 Senators for a total of 535. Additionally, the District of Columbia gets 3 votes as if it were a State, bringing the total to 538. Thus, it takes 270 electoral votes to win a presidential election.

At first this seems straight forward. Sadly, it is not. In the past two centuries Congressmen have proposed over eight-hundred minor changes to the construction of the Electoral College with only one approved. [100]

There are several significant issues with national voting which also ties into the local voting. A key factor is the US concept of freedom which becomes States Rights as mentioned in Chapter One, Freedom. So, each State has the right on how to choose the total number of electors who formally cast votes for President of the US. Some states give the total electoral vote to the candidate with the majority of the state popular vote. For example, Florida has 23 Congressmen and 2 Senators. Each one gets one vote. So, Florida has 25 votes. Thus, the 25 votes go to which ever presidential candidate gets the most votes in Florida. In the 2000 election George Bush won Florida by 537 votes out of almost six-million votes. Therefore, Bush received all 25 electoral votes to reach 271 votes to Gore's 266 votes. Based upon that narrow edge, he won the Presidency even though he lost the total popular vote of the entire US by 543,000 votes. [101]

However, other states give the presidential candidate the electoral votes based upon the percentage each candidate accumulated in the state. For example, in the Florida case, the 25 electoral votes would have been split perhaps 12 going to Bush and 13 going to Gore. But, then the total count for either candidate would have been insufficient to reach at least 270 votes to win the presidency.

100   (Foner 2020)

101   (Wikipedia - United States presidential elections in which the winner lost the popular vote 2020)

Then the House of Representatives, not including the Senate, votes. Most likely that would have been along party lines of either Republican or Democrat. Since the Republicans had the majority, Bush would have won anyway.

The Florida contest went to the Supreme Court of the United States for complicated and contentious legal and political arguments that continue to this day.[102]

Few know that there is no Constitutional requirement on how the States allocate their Electoral College votes. They could have their State Legislature cast the votes without regard to a statewide vote.

A common complaint about the Electoral College is that each State gets at least one vote based upon population plus two votes because each state has two Senators. Thus, each state has a minimum of three votes for President in the Electoral College. Thus small States have more influence than large States.

The other issue that occurs from time to time is when an elector does not vote the way the politics of the election went. That is, the elector votes by one's own conscience and not keeping faith with the electorate. Therefore, the elector is known as a 'faithless elector.' While this has not been an issue, it is possible for it to become one. Only the courts can decide what is legal about a faithless elector.

Voting — Two Houses of Congress

To balance the power between the large states and the small states, the Constitutional Convention created the House of Representatives and the Senate. Each member of the House represents approximately 700,000 people.[103] Each state is guaranteed at least one member in the House. In principle the House proposes legislation and then sends it to the Senate for approval and changes (called reconciliation).

Each State has two Senators for a total of 100 Senators. The Senate also

---

102 (Wikipedia - Bush v Gore 2020)

103 (Wikipedia - United States congressional apportionment 2020)

does legislative work and approves appointments to the President's Cabinet, Federal Courts, military officers, other federal positions, very importantly the Supreme Court.

Voting — Supreme Court

The Senate approves Members of the Supreme Court and lower level Federal Courts for lifetime appointments. Consequently, there is a lot of interest and intrigue in the nomination process. In the past sixty years nominations to the Supreme Court have become increasingly political. If Republicans control the Senate then they will place a judge on the court friendly to business and conservative Christians. The reverse is true if the Senate is Democratic.

For each candidate, teams of Republicans on one side and Democrats on the other search back thirty years through every single document, speech, article, and individual testimonies to either support or destroy the nominee. At times, the process is very regal and at other times exceptionally brutal. They even go back to the high school years.

The aim is to place a person on the Court for at least forty years. That way, even if Republicans or Democrats lose their ability to nominate their candidate, then they will still have their influence on legislation for the next forty years in all the federal levels.

Thus, minority Senators have recently tried to not fill judicial nominations by various procedural moves. Republicans have been very successful with such actions, while Democrats have been quite inept.

Voting — Gerrymandering

In each state voting for a Congressman is a very local function which seems straightforward. However, the party in control of the state legislature in the year following the census determines what the shape of the voting districts will be in. Since the party in control wants to win, it vey carefully draws boundaries to maximize the total number its Party's Representatives in the state.

Thus, knowing the census and the voting affiliation (but theoretically not who voted for whom), ever ten years the boundaries for each Representative are redrawn. This is known as gerrymandering. Some of the districts look like a crescent moon making it almost infeasible for a Representative to know the district. There are a lot of court battles about the gerrymandering which are decided by party affiliated judges who won an election. Thus, the judge might or might not be friendly to a gerrymandering case.

In each state voting for the Senator is a statewide function with the majority vote determining the winner. In some states there are efforts to end the popular vote for Senator and replace it with the local state house choosing the Senator. Thus, if the State house is Republican, then a Republican Senator wins.

Voting — Voter Suppression

Republicans are very aggressively using a variety of tactics to discount Democratic voters. Here are some examples. For a various reasons they remove names from voter registries. For example, if one has not voted in ten years, then the name is removed and only reinstated when the person files again in a timely fashion for the right to vote. People convicted of felony crimes in many states lose the right to vote, although they have served their time. They place an insufficient number of voting machines in parts of districts where minorities live. They claim there might be fraud. However, they create laws and procedures that make it difficult for minorities to vote, in spite of the fact there are very few cases of voter fraud. Although, an appearance of possible fraud occurred when Walden W. O'Dell, the chief executive of Diebold Inc., which manufactured eight percent of the nation's voting machines said, "'I am committed to helping Ohio deliver its electoral votes to the president next ear."[104] This was especially concerning since elections can be won by less than one percent difference.

Other tactics include sending out information that the voting is in a different

104 (Melanie Warner - Machine Politics In the Digital Age 2003)

place or date than it is. Limiting the amount of time for early voting. Also, in the digital age it is easy to broadcast disinformation about the other candidate and issues. Creating so much disinformation that voters of the other side tire of the campaign, just don't vote, or even vote for the wrong candidate.

The Fairness Doctrine of 1949 required television and radio broadcasters to present controversial issues in an honest, equitable, and balanced manner because there were few media outlets.[105] The Republican Reagan administration claimed that hindered the free speech right (First Amendment) of the media. Consequently, in 1987, Congress abandoned the Doctrine with the view that with the advent of many cable networks all views would be aired. Even if the Fairness Doctrine were alive today, it would not cover cable networks and particularly Fox News[106], which claims to be "Fair and Balanced." As a result, the media became aligned with various political parties which a fair number of people believe has led to the extreme polarization of the American public and mind.

Voting — Voter Turnout

The members of the Constitutional Convention wanted to avoid radical swings in the political makeup of the federal government. So, they made the elections for Congressmen every two years, for Senators every six years, and for the Presidents every four years. Thus, the elections are called "mid-term elections" (in the middle of the President's term) and every four years are called "Presidential elections." Since 1948 the percentage of eligible voter turnout for Presidential elections has been from 50% to 60% and in the Midterms about 40%. However, the 2016 Midterm election during Donald Trump's turn in office voter participation jumped to 50% turnout.[107] Consequently, the House of Representatives switched from Republican to Democrat.

105   (Wikipedia - FCC fairness doctrine 2020)

106   (Dan Macguill - Snopes - Did Ronald Reagan Pave the Way for Fox News? 2018)

107   (Michael P. McDonald - National Election Project n.d.)

Thus, when many voters are aligned to one party, winning an election means winning by a few percentage points if that much. Thus, special interest groups and candidates spend millions of dollars to win less than 5% of the votes. On the average a candidate for the US Senate can spend more than $20 million.[108] The total costs of the Presidential races now cost over two billion dollars.[109]

So, with such expensive campaigns, politicians spend significant amount of time raising funds to win. Which means they will listen very carefully to the biggest donors such as Political Action Committees.

Political Action Committees (PAC's)

Virtually every business, religious, or other special interest group forms a Political Action Committee to 'help local, state, and federal legislatures craft legislation, and campaign for or against candidates and issues. Legally there are several types of PAC's each with a set of financial rules. Some are limited to how much money can be raised per individual and others can raise unlimited funds from individuals to include corporations. The latter is becoming more dominant. Some keep donors secret, though the spending must be public.

Various organization form PAC's such as car dealerships, gun enthusiasts, anti-abortion, pro-abortion, anti-union, pro-union, bankers, air traffic controllers, beer manufacturers and distributors, etc. Think of an issue and there is some form of PAC.

These various groups will contribute directly or indirectly to politicians or campaign against politicians. As a result, some campaigns cost millions of dollars, others cost hundreds of millions of dollars, a few like presidential elections cost billions of dollars. Campaign spending is the lifeblood of each politician. Politicians who spend less than an opponent can occasionally win, though that is not the norm.

---

108 (Soo Rin Kim - Open Secrets - The price of winning just got higher, especially in the Senate 2016)

109 (Wikipedia - Campaign finance in the United States 2020)

The result is politicians spend increased time raising funds for the next campaign. As soon as they win or lose an election, they at once start raising funds for the next campaign. Some feel that they spend vastly more time from morning till late evening raising funds than they do crafting legislation. Consequently, they and their staffs rely on PAC's to provide model legislation from experts in their field. For instance, oil companies supply suggestions in the legislative language that is favorable to their interests. Neither the politicians nor their staffs have the time to adequately research the issues, so they find the system helpful. However, other interest groups that do not provide such funding feel that their views are muscled out.

There have been many proposals with some implemented to prevent the corruption of the political process by money. None have effectively succeeded. A key one that did succeed has been Citizens United. The Supreme Court of the United States decreed that corporations have freedom of speech and they can spend unlimited funds on any issue. Consequently, the total amount of spending on campaigns for political offices and issues at all levels of government from the local to the federal level has dramatically increased.

Basically, "He who has the gold, rules." Both political office holders and candidates listen carefully to the PAC's.

Increasingly foreign governments influence the American political process.

Russia & China

The US has meddled in the politics, economics, and religions of Central America, Africa, Asia, and Europe. Yet, many Americans are astounded and upset that Russia, China, Ukraine, North Korea, and other countries meddle in the politics and economics of the US. For some strange reason, many of them feel it is proper for the US to overthrow governments, push for various issues such as human rights, freedom of the speech and the press, monitor voting processes, etc. in other countries. Yet, they take great offense and are surprised when other countries surreptitiously or overtly do the same in the US.

Increasingly without the average American citizen realizing it, other countries supply false information on a variety of topics. The basic aim is sow doubt about the US government's legitimacy and capability as well as supporting candidates and legislation friendly to the foreign entity. With the growing strength of the internet, automated programs called bots can create and spread the information much faster than a few humans can.

Additionally, foreign actors attack corporations and government systems to get financial data on people, corporate and government secrets, influence actions, and shut own vital systems. So far there is no sign that they have influenced the voting counts in elections. But with differences of as little as one percent, it might be difficult to determine if the election was thrown by fraud in the US let alone from Russia,[110] China, North Korea, Ukraine, etc. They are highly skilled people that are shaping the future of the US, and since they do the same in the rest of the world, they are shaping Europe, Africa, Asia, Central American, and South America. With electronic voting who can be sure, especially to find that illusive one percent fraud.

Religion

The liberal clergy are basically uninvolved in the political life of the US. Their interest is in social issues such as homosexuality, education, hunger, global climate change, etc.

On the other hand, the conservative clergy is highly energized for politics and saving the US for the Will of God and for the afterlife. They want the schools, and all the laws and programs from the city, county, state, and nation written in their interpretation of the Bible. They are well funded and highly involved. All political leaders must pass the test of pro-family, anti-homosexuality, anti-abortion, country, guns, Biblical world view, and pro-Israel (land expansion, right to exist, and Jerusalem as the capital of Israel). Those candidates that

---

110   (Thom Hartmann - Does No One Care That 7 Million Votes Were Not Counted? 2017)

do not agree with those issues, do not get their support. Evangelical Prot-estant are 25% [111] of the country, plus portions of other denominations lean to-wards conservative religious views. The total fundamentalist leaning of the country might be about 40%. Just as Pat Buchanan said nearly fifty years earlier would happen.

Fifty years ago, political candidates would mention God and prayer in politi-cal rallies. Over time that has changed to many rallies appearing like religious revival meetings. With the candidates mentioning the issues just listed and the audience cheering wildly.

One would think that Catholics and the Catholic clergy would be involved in the political life of the US because they represented 51 million adults in the US. However, their numbers have declined from 24% in 2007 to 21% in 2014 of the US. Plus, Catholics split their views evenly between conserva-tive and liberal.[112]

Officially, the Church is against abortion, sterilization, all forms of con-traception including vasectomies and hysterectomies, homosexuality, and euthanasia. One unseen quiet area of growing success and power is in the field of health care. They have 15% of the acute care and 10 of the 25 largest health care systems, thus providing one in seven Americans with health care. In many communities they are the only source of medical care.[113] They have more than 600 hospitals and 1,600 long-term care and other health facilities in all 50 states. Thus, the Catholic hospitals are the largest nonprofit health care providers in the nation.[114] Additionally, the Catholic hierarchy is en-couraging members to serve on various medical hospital boards to further

---

111 (Pew Research Center - Religious Landscape Study 2020)

112 (David Masci and Gregory A. Smith - Pew Research Center - 7 facts about American Catholics 2018)

113 (Casey Ross - Catholic hospitals are multiplying, and so is their impact on reproductive health care 2017)

114 (Catholic Health Association of the United States 2020)

increase the reach of Catholic morals. Thus, the Catholic Church is ever so slowly and quietly taking control of the US hospital systems.[115] The aim is to have most US hospitals reflect the Catholic world view.

Finally, the sex abuse scandals have significantly weakened the already waning authority of the clergy and the church's finances. The result is that there are some Catholic leaders that make noise about conservative issues and tend to be somewhat effective. They are not the political force as in the first half of the 20th Century and tend to be on the sidelines. Except however, when joining Conservatives on sexual and end-of-life politics they contribute just enough few percentage points of votes for the Conservative position to win.

So, the Protestant Conservative denominations along with some Catholics, play a significant role in US politics and drive the political landscape like a rising tide towards a conservative theocracy. Nevertheless, the clergy claim that the evil liberal media and religion are persecuting them. They know very well Pat Buchanan's statement, "The Republican Party knows they can't win without us. So, they will do what we tell them."[116]

Meanwhile the liberal clergy is a diverse group quietly watching their congregations, ministerial rosters, schools, and seminaries disappear like the morning fog while turning off the lights, muttering encouraging words for the future, and hoping to reach retirement. For many of them as the congregations dwindle and disappear, the funding for their retirement decreases.

Public Retirement Funds

There are also serious issues with public retirement funds such as State Teacher Retirement programs, State employee retirement programs, the US Post Office, and Social Security and Medicare.

---

115   (Hafner, Katie - As Catholic Hospitals Expand, So Do Limits on Some Procedures 2018r)

116   A statement I heard perhaps Pat Buchanan say in the late 1970's in a TV interview.

For example, in 2006, Congress passed a law requiring the USPS to prefund 75 years' worth of retiree health benefits in the span of ten years—a cost of approximately $110 billion. Although the money was to be set aside for future Post Office retirees, instead the funds were diverted to help pay down the national debt. No other private enterprise or federal agency must prefund retiree health benefits on a comparable timetable. The mandate, using the funds for other purposes, and lack of oversight are responsible for all of USPS's financial losses since 2013.[117]

The same issues plague other public retirement schemes. From time to time some groups make noise to revamp the popular military retirement system.

Similarly, with state retirement funds and Social Security. For instance, the Federal Government uses the accumulated reserve funds for other governmental activities such as the military. Part of the issue is that the retirement funds are collected and then the various state and federal government legislatures say, "We can better utilize the funds that are just sitting there. When the time comes, we will pay it back." That does not happen. Instead there are screams of mismanagement and then blaming the US Post Office or Social Security or someone else for the problems.

Though some do make proposals to switch the systems to privatization. That is, put the funds into various stock market schemes. Which artificially raises the value of the stock market benefiting for a while many stockholders, corporations, and corporate executives.

So, politicians 'kick the can down the road' for some other politician to handle. Similarly, what they do with global climate change.

Global Climate Change

The Federal Government is effectively ignoring and actively suppressing mentioning and doing any actions to avert global climate change. The

---

117   (Peter Defazio - US Congressman 2020)

Republicans consider that man-made global climate change is a massive hoax. That the climate naturally changes. That opening of the Arctic seaways will help businesses because there will be easier movement of ships and access to the vast oil fields currently underneath the polar ice and snow. The Trump administration bars any mention of Global Climate Change, prohibits access to supporting data, and dismisses those that violate such directives or publicly speak out.

On the other hand, scientists, and many Democrats meekly state that the climate is changing. Occasionally they wake up, but then are preoccupied with raising funds to win elections, spend time fighting for civil rights, and other issues that they are concerned about.

However, quietly many companies and local governments are doing what they can to improve carbon emissions and going green. At best, the US is making some but insufficient progress on Global Climate Change.

The US ignores, that there will be massive disruptions as the Tibetan glaciers supply less year-round water to rivers flowing into China, India, Pakistan, Bangladesh, Cambodia, Vietnam, and Laos. Currently, increasing populations and industrial demands are creating water shortages in that region. In fifty years, China controlling the Tibetan Plateau will determine the fate of non-Chinese friendly countries.

The US government ignores that its vast interior farmlands in less than a hundred years has the distinct possibility of becoming arid and effectively impossible to feed the US let alone export to the world. The weather will become more variable, with periods of intense rain and drought, high and low heat. There will be adverse effects upon the crops and livestock, with increases in pathogens, pests, and weeds.[118]

Global Climate Change is the single most challenging issue facing the US and the world. Yet, the US business, political, and religious leadership effectively

---

118   (Union of Concerne Scientists - Climate Change and Agriculture 2019)

ignore it, deny it, and passes the issue to the next generations. Effectively the US will be killing millions of Americans and billions of people in the world. They effectively don't care.

Thus, the political intrigue of US business, political, and religious leadership puts America at the crossroads for the future.

Chapter 9

America at the Crossroads

Americans are at the crossroads of what it means to be an American. Fundamentalist Christians and Republicans say they are waging war for the very soul of America. They want to go back to the Christian roots that made America great. Republicans want to free America from the burdensome rule of the Federal and State governments and international organizations that *enfeebles people and hinders corporations.*

Fundamentalist Christians are very effectively implementing their very Conservative views in the US. They want very public displays of "In God We Trust," on State and Federal vehicles, buildings, money, and documents. Additionally, they want prayer in public gatherings such as football games, schools, political rallies, courts, legislative sessions, and military events. Most importantly, they want State and Federal laws to be based upon Judeo-Christian values as stated in the Bible, which they also want as the official book of US and each of the fifty states.

Meanwhile liberal Christians, humanists, and secularists are barely aware of these actions, have little interest in politics, and thus ineffective in implementing their own views. So, liberalism quietly declines while dreamily believing that demographics and the future is on their side.

Republicans, with the support of fundamentalist Christians, want to eliminate, downsize, or privatize Federal and State bureaucracies such as

Social Security
Medicare, Medicaid
Department of Education
Internal Revenue Service
Environmental Protection Agency

Obamacare

Department of Energy[119]

Federal Election Assistance Agency[120]

Office of Personnel Management[121]

U.S. Immigration and Customs Enforcement (ICE)[122]

Internal Revenue Service, Department of Commerce

Department of Housing and Urban Development[123]

Consumer Financial Protection Bureau[124]

The US Post Office[125]

Defense Nuclear Facilities Safety Board[126]

Veterans Affairs, Bureau of the Census

McGovern-Dole International Food for Education

Rural Business and Cooperative Services

Economic Development Administration

Manufacturing Extension Partnership

21st Century Learning Centers

Gaining Early Awareness and Readiness for Undergraduate Programs

Agency for Health Care Research and Quality

Advanced Research Projects Agency

---

119   (Brad Pulmer - Vox - Rick Perry once wanted to abolish the Energy Department. Trump picked him to run it. 2016)

120   (Eric Katz, Senior Correspondent - Government Executive - House Republicans Want to Eliminate Federal Election Assistance Agency 2017)

121   (Lisa Rein & Damian Palleta, Washington Post - If Trump has his way, this major federal agency is on the way out 2019)

122   (Wikipedia - Abolish ICE 2020)

123   (Matthew Flemming, Roll Call - The 5 Agencies Ted Cruz Would Cut 2015)

124   (Housing Wire - Republicans move to abolish CFPB 2019)

125   (Bill Prascall Jr, Washington Monthly - Congress Is Sabotaging Your Post Office 2019)

126   (Patrick Malone & R. Jeffry Smith - GOP chair of nuclear safety agency secretly urges Trump to abolish it 2018)

> The National Wildlife Refuge Fund
>
> The Global Climate Change Initiative
>
> NASA Office of Education
>
> The Chemical Safety Board
>
> The Corporation For Public Broadcasting
>
> The Institute for Museum and Library Services
>
> The Legal Services Corporation
>
> The National Endowment for the Arts
>
> The National Endowment for the Humanities
>
> The Neighborhood Reinvestment Corporation
>
> The Denali Commission
>
> The Delta Regional Authority and
>
> The Northern Border Regional Commission
>
> The U.S. Trade and Development Agency
>
> The Woodrow Wilson International Center for Scholars[127]
>
> Numerous civil and human rights initiatives[128]
>
> Fair Pay and Safe Workplaces Executive Order[129]

as well privatization of infrastructure such as roads, tunnels, bridges, public lands, and National Parks. Plus, more not listed. The "Overthrow Project" has been on many groups instrumental in this effort.[130]

They also want to turn away from world organizations such as the World Health Organization, UNESCO, Transpacific Trade Partnership, North American Free Trade Agreement (though replaced with a different name), and sometimes NATO, and other international organizations. They consider

127 (Brett Samuels, The Hill - The 22 agencies and programs Trump's budget would eliminate 2018)

128 (The Leadership Council On Civil and Human Rights - Trump Administration Civil and Human Rights Rollbacks 2020)

129 (The Leadership Council On Civil and Human Rights - Trump Administration Civil and Human Rights Rollbacks 2017)

130 (Herbert J. Gans, The Nation - This Is How the Republican Party Plans to Destroy the Federal Government 2017)

these as part of the New World Order which aims to make the world including the United States socialistic.

Additionally, they use several ways to dramatically reduce the federal government. Examples are, "Starve the Beast," by not funding or reduce funding of disliked programs. Move bureaucracies from Washington, DC to other places thus forcing people to quit or retire. Eliminate two to ten regulations for every new one. Have "States Rights" be a driving theme of freedom by giving States block grants to do as they please while reducing or ending federal activities. Bypass Congress by extensively using Executive Decrees. The intent is to reduce the Federal government. That is to "make the federal government so small that one can flush it down the toilette."[131]

However, they will keep and strengthen law and order programs such as the military, Homeland Security, police, and privatize prisons as well as gain control over all branches of the Federal and State governments.[132]

Essentially, Republicans believe in survival of the fittest and that all who want to work will find good paying jobs. Those that do not want to work can starve. They believe at their core, that implementing extremely limited government with a very limited social safety net, embracing the Prosperity Gospel, and basing American values upon Christian Fundamentalism will create a prosperous, wealthy, strong, and secure America independent of foreign corrupting socialistic countries.

The language Republicans use, and their emotions are of war against liberalism, otherwise known as the "L word."[133] It is a language liberals and Democrats dislike and ignore at their peril. As Arthur Brooks, President of the American Enterprise Institute, a leading Republican think tank said,[134]

131   (Wikiquote - Grover Norquist 2019)

132   (Herbert J. Gans, The Nation - This Is How the Republican Party Plans to Destroy the Federal Government 2017)

133   (Jennifer Rubin - Washington Post - George H.W. Bush and the 'L' word 2018)

134   (Arthur Brooks at CPAC: Reward the makers 2012)

President Obama is certainly not shy about making economic policy a matter almost entirely about morality. After all, what else was he doing when he said Jesus would support the Buffett rule? Believers in the wonder-working power of economic freedom can either make the moral case (as well as the economic one), or retreat at the first sound of a liberal moral argument. My approach is, to quote (Bruce Springsteen), "No retreat, baby, no surrender." [135]

By the way, "The Buffett Rule" is named after Warren Buffett, an American investor and one of the richest men in the world, who believed it was wrong that rich people, like himself, could pay less in federal taxes, as a portion of income, than the middle class, and voiced support for increased income taxes on the wealthy. The rule would implement a higher minimum tax rate for taxpayers in the highest income bracket, to ensure that they do not pay a lower percentage of income in taxes than less-affluent Americans. The Obama White House further defined the Rule as everyone making over a million dollars a year would pay at least 30 percent income tax. [136]

Meanwhile, liberal Christians and Democrats for fifty years have believed that as more women and minorities enter politics, Democrats will automatically have power to preserve the New Deal and to enhance social safety net programs. But they have not energized their hearts enough nor thought out their plans enough to win over enough average people they are trying to support. They meekly stand against the Republicans and do not clearly and simply say what they stand for. Republicans lay out their strategy and the Democrats in general ignore it, don't believe it, or are too incompetent to take action.

Perhaps the very programs that created the social safety net made the Democrats and many other Americans lazy. Just as Republicans have said, "*The net*

---

135   The title "No Surrender," is from the Album, "Born in the USA." (Wikipedia - No Surrender (Song) 2020)

136   (Wikipedia - Buffett Rule 2019)

majority of Americans are takers and not makers"[137] *and, "...we will reward the makers, not the takers."*[138] That language is simple and clear and by the way helps define Democrats who pay no attention to the labels Republicans put on them.

So, Republicans strongly and clearly say that America will create wealth through faith in Jesus, implementing Judeo-Christian laws, and free the American capitalistic spirit from US and international oppressive laws. This will create a country where Americans are free to work or starve, are independent of international intrigue, and free from the global climate change hoax.

Meanwhile, Democrats struggle to articulate a sharp vision of creating an America that is "happy, healthy, wealthy, and wise, through work and love." Or some simple, clear, easy to understand statement. For example, Republicans have MAGA, "Make America Great Again."

So, Republicans and Democrats have two distinct views of

Freedom and opportunity

For about two centuries the world viewed the United States as the symbol of freedom and opportunity. With work and with some luck, one could create a nice life that would be free of demagogues, tyrants, discrimination, religious and economic oppression.

The Statue of Liberty is the symbol of freedom. The ideal to be free as an American appears in politics, movies, books, media, religion, and education. Though that was not true for slaves, American Indians, and the millions living in poverty. But even the later lived with the sense that freedom was possible and that they had it. A few like Andrew Carnegie, Thomas Edison, George Vanderbilt, and others went from nothing to creating vast wealth. They and similar others became an inspiration for millions of Americans.

---

137 (The Week - Don't listen to Paul Ryan: The GOP is still the party of makers and takers 2014)

138 (Arthur Brooks at CPAC: Reward the makers 2012)

To understand an American, is to understand that freedom is in the very blood and bones of American ideals, mythology, psyche, training, and breath. It is fundamental in a way of thinking that is somewhat elusive to Europeans, Asians, Africans, and South Americans. Nevertheless, that sense of freedom inspires millions of people around the world to work and live in the United States – the Land of the Free.

However, this sense of freedom creates a tension of being individuals within a society. The emphasis tends to be highly individualistic where a person is free to do whatever one wants. The fewer the laws the better. The fewer the restrictions on property the better.

On the other hand, an American ideal is Law and Order. There is a deep desire to have a society that follows the law but somehow allows people to be free so long as their freedom does not impinge upon themselves. But many people are willing to have their views be the law of the land and impinge upon the freedom of others.

Thus, Republicans and Democrats have different views of freedom and law and order.

Republicans and Democrats also have different view of what man-made political and economic institutions should be that underlie economic success (or lack of it). [139] Republicans focus intently upon an extremely limited government with maximum freedom for corporations. They call government burdensome and partner with conservative religious groups which also seek to limit the freedoms of individuals. To get their programs funded, they borrow and spend.

Meanwhile Democrats focus on a broad range of human rights which means limiting corporate and religious power in order to have inclusive institutions that serve the whole nation and not just the top one to five percent. To

---

139 (Daron Acemoglu, James A. Robinson - Why Nations Fail: The Origins of Power, Prosperity, and Poverty 2013)

achieve their programs, they tax and spend.

The result is a muddled fiscal structure that is not economically nor physically healthy for the American people.

Perhaps this political and religious conflict contributes to,

An Underlying Issue

Without work and love most people find life is not satisfying, lacks meaning, and society decays. For fifty years American business, political, and religious leadership and American consumers unwittingly encouraged or silently supported the evisceration of lower- and middle-class jobs. American consumers bought products solely based on price, which forced businesses to ruthlessly cut costs. Thus the prices of goods were cheaper which raised their standard of living until many of their jobs were also moved overseas to lower cost production areas or businesses automated jobs away. Adding to the turmoil were corporate takeover artists that bought companies, grabbed the wealthy parts, often declared bankruptcy, cut jobs, made a fortune, and then walked away rich.

Meanwhile more Americans took legal and illegal drugs creating a health epidemic, whiled away hours watching television or playing video games. Many lost the will or skill to work and love. On the one hand American businesses created more wealth for many while dramatically adversely impacting the lives of millions who did not or could not figure out a way to increase their prosperity.

Thus, many Americans became…

Neurotic

Americans as a group desire to be happy and sufficiently wealthy to do what they want. But as a group they are neither healthy nor wise. They gravitate towards whatever pleases them while believing that whatever they want they are free to have. So, they consume unhealthy foods. Spend money without regard to debt both personally and nationally. Desire to be physically fit, yet as a nation they are obese[140] couch potatoes watching hours of mindless television and buff professional athletes. They take magic diets to lose weight and then gain it right back and are heavier. Unwilling to take personal responsibility for themselves, they demand legal and illegal pills to cure their ills. They blame others for their problems but are unwilling to do the work needed to cure their ills. They are like drunks riding a horse. At first, they ride upright. Then the slide to the right, then pull upwards and slide to the left. They go through life flopping back and forth.[141]

American society lacks common values shared by individuals, families, groups, and states, and the nation. The US is polarized with groups wanting their 'correct' views imposed upon all. Instead of political, business, religious, and educational leaders doing the difficult work of dialoguing, they instead create divisions and strive to win. Republicans know they are right and are doing the best for the country and those who disagree are the *evil enemy*. An enemy to destroy by any means possible. Their aim is to win by all means possible. On the other hand, Democrats tend to view the other half as misguided ignorant people. With such polarization it will be difficult to create a nation built upon tolerance for diversity. As the old motto said, "Out of many, one." That has faded from the American dream and consciousness.

All this happens because interest political, business, and religious groups work to impose their views on a broad diverse society. Republicans believe that government governs best when it governs least. That people and corporations are free to do what they want, when they want. The vision of government is that of the later 1700's and early 1800's. A simple government for a simpler time.

---

140   (Mark Hertling, Lieutant General - Obesity is a National Security Issue 2012)

141   Adapted from Martin Luther writing about being a Christian. (Christian History Institute - The Drunk Peasant 2017)

On the other hand, Democrats believe that the issues confronting the US and the world are way more complicated than two hundred years ago. That the government, laws, economics, education, religion, and citizens must change to meet the current times, increased diversity, and international issues. Unfortunately, Democrats struggle to articulate simple clear messages that resonate with the average American.

So, will the Unites States

Be a Christian theocracy
or
a secular society?

Be run by corporations
or
a dynamic mix of socialism and capitalism?

It appears that the US is heading towards a conservative anti-science theocratic society dominated by corporations. The Republicans have dedicated radio, TV, Internet education and news programs, hats, tee shirts, flags, NRA, Heritage Foundation, American Enterprise Institute, Hillsdale College, Liberty University, thousands of fundamentalist churches, a huge powerful daily Internet system, a gargantuan fund raising machine, and vast energy and enthusiasm. For the 2020 campaign season they have accumulated $600 billion to the Democrats $450 billion.[142] Additionally, Republicans have massively more amounts of dark money support from corporations and foreign entities[143] than the Democrats do.

Meanwhile, liberal Democratic leadership and populace dream of recapturing their vision of the US without explaining it in simple coherent English to the average American. They have the same type of institutions just mentioned

142   (Ballotpedia - Party committee fundraising, 2019-2020 2020)

143   (Lee Fang - The Intercept - Foreign-Funded Dark-Money Groups Lobby IRS to Repeal Remaining Reporting Requirements 2020) plus numerous other articles on Dark Money for both Republicans and Democrats. Though more so for Republicans.

that the Republicans have. But those institutions lack the vibrancy, simple clarity, and depth of thought that the Republicans have. However, there are some exceptions such as Thom Hartman, Rachael Maddow, Washington Post, New York Times, and a few others.

Yet, the US can create a set of shared values that views diversity as a strength, work as an honor, money as a resource, broad science based education as a necessity, physical and mental fitness as a duty, etc. What it needs are statesmen to reiterate what the US in the modern age as "a society of individuals" stands for. At this point, only the Republicans clearly articulate that view; however, at the expense of the middle and lower classes.

Will the USA be

Run by corporations

with a fundamentalist Christian theocracy

or

A blend of capitalism, socialism, and secularism

In the age of Trump?

Bibliography

Andreae, Jacob; Chemnitz, Martin. "Chief Articles of Faith." *The Book of Concord.* 1530. http://bookofconcord.org/augsburgconfession.php (accessed March 14, 2018).

Admin. "Difference Between Faith and Hope." *Ipedia.* December 15, 2015. http://pediaa.com/difference-between-faith-and-hope/ (accessed March 19, 2018).

Ahlstrom, Sydney. *A Religious History of the American People.* New Haven and London: Yale University Press, 1975.

AIG. "What Is the Meaning of Life?" *Answers in Genesis.* n.d. https://answersingenesis.org/what-is-the-meaning-of-life/ (accessed March 27, 2018).

ALEC - American Legislative Exchange Council. "ALEC - About - Task Force - Home." *ALEC.org.* n.d. https://www.alec.org/about/ (accessed May 7, 2020).

Ali, M. Amir, Ph.D. "Forgiveness." *Institute of Islamic Information and Education.* February 24, 2006. http://www.iiie.net/forgiveness/ (accessed February 19, 2018).

All Types of STDs and STIs, STD Symptoms, STD Pictures, STD Treatment. n.d.

Al-Munajjid, Sheikh Muhammed Salih. "Explaining human suffering and why Allaah does not prevent it ." *Islam Question & Answer.* November 11, 1998. https://islamqa.info/en/answers/2850/explaining-human-suffering-and-why-allaah-does-not-prevent-it (accessed October 22, 2018).

Altucher, James. "The Six Things The Most Productive People Do Every Day." *The Medium.* May 28, 2018. https://medium.com/the-mission/the-six-things-the-most-productive-people-do-every-day-fba2fe17ed45 (accessed May 281, 2018).

Alumkal, Antony. *Paranoid Science - The Christian Right's War on Reality.* New York: New York University Press, 2017.

American Journal of Nursing. "Growing Number of Catholic-Run Hospitals Raises Concerns." *American Journal of Nursing.* Dec 2019. https://journals.lww.com/ajnonline/Fulltext/2019/12000/Growing_Number_of_Catholic_Run_Hospitals_Raises.12.aspx (accessed May 1, 2020).

American Psychological Association - Gun Violence: Prediction, Prevention, and Policy . "Gun Violence: Prediction, Prevention, and Policy ." *American Psychological Association.* 2013. https://www.apa.org/pubs/info/reports/gun-violence-prevention (accessed May 26, 2020).

Anonymous. "religous authority: Hinduism." *ReligionFacts.com.* November 19, 2016. http://www.religionfacts.com/hinduism/authority (accessed March 13, 2018).

Antony J. Blinken and Robert Kagan - Brookings - 'America First' is only making the world worse. Here's a better approach. "'America First' is only making the world worse. Here's a better approach." *Brookings.* Jan 4, 2019. https://www.brookings.edu/blog/order-from-chaos/2019/01/04/america-first-is-only-making-the-world-worse-heres-a-better-approach/ (accessed May 25, 2020).

Arendt, Hannah. *The Life of the Mind.* San Diego New Yor London: A Harvest Book a division of Harcourt Brace & Company, 1977.

—. *The Origins of Totalitarianism.* New York: Harcourt, Inc, 1966.

Arkush, Allan. "Immortality: Belief in a Bodiless Existence - Everlasting life was not always guaranteed to the Jewish soul." *My Jewish Learning.* n.d. https://www.myjewishlearning.com/article/immortality-belief-in-a-bodiless-existence/ (accessed August 3, 2018).

—. "Immortality: Belief in a Bodiless Existence." *My Jewish Learning.* n.d. https://www.myjewishlearning.com/article/immortality-belief-in-a-bodiless-existence/ (accessed March 2, 2018).

Armstrong, Karen. *The Battle For God.* New York: Alfred A. Knopf, 2000.

Arsenal| HistoryNet. "CH-47C Chinook Helicopter." *historynet.com.* n.d. https://www.google.com/search?q=Vietnam+Chinook+helicopter+pictures&newwindow=1&client=firefox-b-1-d&tbm=isch&source=iu&ictx=1&fir=ndcw-ZaPVJBMrdM%253A%252CU6BfELmRJGmQSM%252C_&vet=1&usg=AI4_-kQNJIj6shgIpyLwj-58BAF4qCnmuQ&sa=X&ved=2ahUKEwja5Pm-6JjiAhUE658K (accessed May 15, 2019).

Arthur Brooks at CPAC: Reward the makers, not the takers. "Arthur Brooks at CPAC: Reward the makers, not the takers." *Faith and Public Life.* Feb 10, 2012. https://faithandpubliclife.com/arthur-brooks-at-cpac-reward-the-makers-not-the-takers/ (accessed May 30, 2020).

ArtLords. "Warlord with Pencils." *ArtLords.* n.d. https://www.artlords.co (accessed August 2, 2019).

"Attributes of God." *All About.* 2018. https://www.allaboutgod.com/attributes-of-god.htm (accessed October 5, 2018).

Ballotpedia - Party committee fundraising, 2019-2020. "Party committee fundraising, 2019-2020." *Ballotpedia.* May 21, 2020. https://ballotpedia.org/Party_committee_fundraising,_2019-2020 (accessed May 30, 2020).

Bauer, Susan Wise. *The Well-Educated Mind - A Guide to the Classical Educaton You Never Had.* New York: W.W. Norton & Company, Inc, 2016.

Beit-Halachmi, Rabbi Rachel Sabath. "The Experience and Nearness of God." *My Jewish Learning.* n.d. https://www.myjewishlearning.com/article/the-experience-and-nearness-of-god/ (accessed March 1, 2018).

Beltran, Victoria. "Sex Education…With Pleasure ." *TEDxUSFSP.* January 6, 2016. https://www.youtube.com/watch?v=R-gwxS-7h9o (accessed December 5, 2018).

Bercot, David. "Love Without Condition." *History of the Early Church.* n.d. http://www.earlychurch.com/unconditional-love.php (accessed November 14, 2016).

—. "What was the early church like?" *History of the Early Church.* n.d. http://earlychurch.com/index-old.html (accessed November 14, 2016).

Berger, Jonah. *Invisible Influence - The Hidden Forces That Shape Behavior.* New York: Simon & Shuster, 2016 June.

Berman, Robby, and Samantha Lee. "When You Can't Afford to Make a Mistake, This'll Keep You Sharp (20 cognitive biases in a chart that could keep you from making a bad decision)." *Big Think.* April 19, 2016. https://bigthink.com/robby-berman/a-chart-of-brain-busting-cognitive-biases-hang-it-on-your-wall (accessed September 23, 2018).

Bhat, Tehreem. "Do Muslims believe that there is no way but Islam to experience God?" *Quroa.* March 18, 2015. https://www.quora.com/Do-Muslims-believe-that-there-is-no-way-but-Islam-to-experience-God (accessed March 1, 2018).

Bhikkhu, Thanissaro. "All About Change." *A Theravada Library* . 2004. https://www.accesstoinsight.org/lib/authors/thanissaro/change.html (accessed March 21, 2018).

Bill Prascall Jr, Washington Monthly - Congress Is Sabotaging Your Post Office . "Congress Is Sabotaging Your Post Office ." *Washington Monthly.* April/May 2019. https://washingtonmonthly.com/magazine/april-may-june-2019/congress-is-sabotaging-your-post-office/ (accessed May 30, 2020).

Blanchard, LInda. "Who Is The Ultimate Authority?" *Secular Buddhist Association.* July 23, 2012. http://secularbuddhism.org/2012/07/23/who-is-the-ultimate-authority/ (accessed March 13, 2018).

Blitz, Matt. "The Articles of Confederation: The Constitution Before the Constitution." *Today I Found Out.* Dec 24, 2013. http://www.todayifoundout.com/index.php/2013/12/articles-confederation-constitution-constitution/ (accessed May 5, 2020).

Bloom, A. "Buddhist Studies: Glossary of Terms." *Buddha Dharma Education Association & BuddhaNet.* 2018. https://www.buddhanet.net/e-learning/dharmadata/fdd29.htm (accessed March 19, 2018).

Blumenthal, David. "REPENTANCE AND FORGIVENESS." *David Blumenthal's HomePage.* n.d. http://www.js.emory.edu/BLUMENTHAL/Repentance.html (accessed January 29, 2019).

Boroditsky, Lera. "How language shapes the way we think." *TED.* May 2, 2018. https://www.youtube.com/watch?v=RKK7wGAYP6k (accessed November 19, 2018).

Brad Pulmer - Vox - Rick Perry once wanted to abolish the Energy Department. Trump picked him to run it. "Rick Perry once wanted to abolish the Energy Department. Trump picked him to run it." *Vox.* Dec 13, 2016. https://www.vox.com/energy-and-environment/2016/12/13/13936210/rick-perry-energy-department-trump (accessed May 30, 2020).

BrainyMedia, Inc. "Max Muller Quotes." *Brainy Quote.* n.d. https://www.brainyquote.com/quotes/max_muller_326659 (accessed December 10, 2018).

Brett Samuels, The Hill - The 22 agencies and programs Trump's budget would eliminate. "The 22 agencies and programs Trump's budget would eliminate." *The Hill.* Feb 18, 2018. https://thehill.com/homenews/administration/373441-the-federal-programs-trump-proposes-cutting-in-2019-budget (accessed May 30, 2020).

Brown, Raymond E. *An Introdtion to the New Testament (abridged).* New Haven & London: Yale University Press, 2016.

Bruckner, Pascal. "Condemned to Joy: The Western cult of happiness is a mirthless enterprise." *City Journal.* Winter 2011. https://www.city-journal.org/html/condemned-joy-13355.html (accessed February 8, 2019).

Buchanan, Patrick J. *The Death of the West.* New York: Thomas Dunn Books, 2002.

Buchholz, Katharina. "statista." *The Trans-Atlantic Slave Trade Uprooted Millions.* Aug 20, 2019. https://www.statista.com/chart/19068/trans-atlantic-slave-trade-by-country-region/ (accessed May 1, 2020).

"Buddha." *The Pursuit of Happiness - Bringing the science of happiness to life.* n.d. http://www.pursuit-of-happiness.org/history-of-happiness/buddha/ (accessed March 27, 2018).

Burton, Tara Isabella. "This poll asked Americans if they believe in God. The answers were fascinating." *Vox*. April 26, 2018. https://www.vox. com/2018/4/26/17282284/pew-americans-god-religion-study-faith-identity (accessed April 27, 2018).

C.S.Lewis. *God in the Dock (Essays on Theology and Ethics)*. Grand Rapids, Michigan/ Cambridge, U.K.: William B. Erdmans Publishing company, 1970.

Caruso, Steve. "The Lord's Prayer in Galilean Aramaic." *The Aramaic New Testament - Galilean New Testament in the Context of Early Christianity*. n.d. http://aramaicnt.org/ articles/the-lords-prayer-in-galilean-aramaic/ (accessed November 13, 2016).

Casey Ross - Catholic hospitals are multiplying, and so is their impact on repro- ductive health care. "Catholic hospitals are multiplying, and so is their impact on reproductive health care." *STAT*. Sep 14, 2017. https://www.statnews. com/2017/09/14/catholic-hospitals-reproductive-health-care/ (accessed May 25, 2020).

Catholic Health Association of the United States. "Facts Statistics." *Catholic Health Association of the United States*. Jan 2020. https://www.chausa.org/about/about/ facts-statistics (accessed May 25, 2020).

Catron, Mandy Len. *how to fall in love with anyone*. New York, New York: Simon & Shuster, 2017.

Cavendish, Marshall. *Islamic Beliefs, Practices, and Cultures*. Malaysia: Marshall Caven- dish Reference, 2011.

Chafer, Lewis Sperry. *Systematic Theology Vol 1-8*. Dallas, Texas: Dallas Seminary Press, 1947 Eleventh Edition 1973.

Christian History Institute - The Drunk Peasant. "The Drunk Peasant." *Christian History Institute*. Jun 17, 2017. https://christianhistoryinstitute.org/blog/post/ the-drunk-peasant/ (accessed May 30, 2020).

Chugh, Anmol. "As per Buddhism, what is the purpose of life?" *Quroa*. February 14, 2016. https://www.quora.com/As-per-Buddhism-what-is-the-purpose-of-life (accessed March 27, 2018).

Church of England. "Section XIV of Saving Faith." *Center for Reformed Theology and Apologetics*. 1646. http://www.reformed.org/documents/index.html?main- frame=http://www.reformed.org/documents/westminster_conf_of_faith.html (accessed March 14, 2018).

Ciara Torres-Spelliscy - "American Bar Assocition". "Does "We the People" Include Corporations?" *American Bar Association*. n.d. https://www.americanbar.org/ groups/crsj/publications/human_rights_magazine_home/we-the-people/ we-the-people-corporations/ (accessed May 7, 2020).

Clear, James. *Atomic Habits: An Easy & Proven Way to Build Good Habits & Break Bad Ones*. New York: Penguin Random House, 2018.

Cleveland Clinic. *Female Reproductive System* . February 5, 2019. https://my.cleveland- clinic.org/health/articles/9118-female-reproductive-system (accessed March 27, 2019).

Cole, Wayne. "America First - The Battle Against Intervention 1940-1941." *Amazon*. November 4, 2008. America First - The Battle Against Intervention 1940-1941 (accessed April 13, 2019).

Conroy, Alec M. "File:Relationship between synoptic gospels.png." *Wikimedia Commons.* May 13, 2012. https://commons.wikimedia.org/wiki/File:Relationship_between_synoptic_gospels.png (accessed June 16, 2019).

—. "File:Synoptic problem two source colored.png." *Wikimedia Commons.* November 28, 2007. https://commons.wikimedia.org/wiki/File:Synoptic_problem_two_source_colored.png (accessed June 16, 2019).

Conservativ Political Action Conference - Agenda. "CPAC2020 - Agenda." *Conservative Political Action Conference.* Feb 26, 2020. https://links.conservative.org/cpac/agenda/cpac-2020-agenda-0d3jsA.pdf (accessed May 28, 2020).

Conservative Political Action Conference . "CPAC2020." *American Conservative Union CPAC.* 2020. https://cpac.conservative.org/ (accessed May 28, 2020).

Copyright: Freedom Studio. "Jesus knocking on the door, original oil painting on canvas; Image ID:264711281." *Shutterstock.* n.d. http://www.shutterstock.com/pic-264711281/stock-photo-jesus-knocking-on-the-door-original-oil-painting-on-canvas.html (accessed November 6, 2016).

Corey, Benjamin L. "To Those Christians Who Say, "God Doesn't Give Us More Than We Can Handle"." *Patheos Progressive Christian.* October 12, 2017. http://www.patheos.com/blogs/formerlyfundie/christians-say-god-doesnt-give-us-can-handle/#comment-3861255192 (accessed October 22, 2018).

Costa, Pam. "Reclaiming Female Sexual Desire." *TedX Palo Alto.* June 5, 2018. https://www.youtube.com/watch?v=0Sn_UhcXZm4 (accessed November 15, 2018).

Council of Nicea. "The Nicene Creed." *creeds.net.* 325 AD. https://www.creeds.net/ancient/nicene.htm (accessed March 14, 2018).

Daley, Kevin. "Roberts, Liberal Justices Wary of Trump Exemptions to Birth Control Mandate." *The Morning Beacon.* My 6, 2020. https://freebeacon.com/courts/roberts-liberal-justices-wary-of-trump-exemptions-to-birth-control-mandate/?utm_source=actengage&utm_campaign=FreedomMail&utm_medium=email (accessed May 7, 2020).

Dan Macguill - Snopes - Did Ronald Reagan Pave the Way for Fox News? "Did Ronald Reagan Pave the Way for Fox News?" *Snopes.* Jan 26, 2018. https://www.snopes.com/fact-check/ronald-reagan-fairness-doctrine/ (accessed May 22, 2020).

David Masci and Gregory A. Smith - Pew Research Center - 7 facts about American Catholics. "7 facts about American Catholics." *Pew Research Center - FactTank News in the Numbers.* Oct 10, 2018. https://www.pewresearch.org/fact-tank/2018/10/10/7-facts-about-american-catholics/ (accessed May 25, 2020).

David Pattison -Social Security Office of Retirment and Disability - Social Security Trust Fund Cash Flows and Reserves. "Social Security Trust Fund Cash Flows and Reserves." *Social Security Office of Retirment and Disability - Social Security Trust Fund Cash Flows and Reserves - Social Security Bulletin, Vol. 75, No. 1, 2015.* 2015. https://www.ssa.gov/policy/docs/ssb/v75n1/v75n1p1.html (accessed May 27, 2020).

David Taylor - The Guardian - Project Blitz: the legislative assault by Christian nationalists to reshape America. "Project Blitz: the legislative assault by Christian nationalists to reshape America." *The Guardian.* Jun 4, 2018. https://www.theguardian.com/world/2018/jun/04/project-blitz-the-legislative-assault-by-christian-nationalists-to-reshape-america (accessed May 28, 2020).

Dawkins, Richard. "The Genius of Charles Darwin." *The Genius of Charles Darwin.* Athena IWC Media Limited 2008, 2008.

Deepak, Chopra, and Leonard Mlodinow. *War of the Worldviews - Science vs Spirituality.* New York: Crown Publishing Group, a division of Random House, In, 2011.

Denning, Stephanie. "Dollar Shave Club Founder: Why Life Is Defined By Choices." *Forbes.* May 31, 2018. https://www.forbes.com/sites/stephaniedenning/2018/05/31/dollar-shave-club-founder-why-life-is-defined-by-choices/#419614495abd (accessed June 7, 2018).

Dhammika, Van S. "Nearly all religions have some kind of holy writings or Bible. What is the Buddhist holy book?" *Good Questions With Good Answers.* n.d. http://www.buddhanet.net/ans66.htm (accessed March 13, 018).

Dollar Times - Calculate the Value of dollars in today's times. "Calculate the Value of dollars in today's times." *Dollar Times.* 2020. https://www.dollartimes.com/inflation/inflation.php?amount=100&year=1925 (accessed May 28, 2020).

Drane, John. "The Bible." *BBC - Religions.* July 12, 2011. http://www.bbc.co.uk/religion/religions/christianity/texts/bible.shtml (accessed October 15, 2018).

Dubner, Stephen J, and Steven D Levitt. *Think Like A Freak.* New York: Harper Collins Publisher, 2014.

Duhigg, Charles. "Wealthy Successful and Miserable." *The Future of Work - The New York Tmes Magazine.* February 22, 2019. https://www.nytimes.com/interactive/2019/02/21/magazine/elite-professionals-jobs-happiness.html (accessed February 22, 2019).

Durant, Will and Ariel. *The Story of Civilization.* 11 vols. New York: Simon & Shuster, 1975.

Ehrenreich, Barbara. *Natural Causes.* New York Boston: Twelve, 2018.

Ehrman, Bart D. *God's Problem, How the Bible Fails to Answer Our most Important Question - Why We Suffer.* New York: Harper Collins, 2008.

Ehrman, Bart. *God's Problem.* New Hork: HarperCollins, 2008.

Encyclopedia Britannica. "Hinduism - Religion." *Encyclopedia Britannica.* February 7, 2018. https://www.britannica.com/topic/Hinduism/Introduction (accessed October 23, 2018).

Eric Katz, Senior Correspondent - Government Executive - House Republicans Want to Eliminate Federal Election Assistance Agency . "House Republicans Want to Eliminate Federal Election Assistance Agency ." *Government Executive.* Jun 30, 2017. https://www.govexec.com/management/2017/06/house-republicans-want-eliminate-federal-election-assistance-agency/139123/ (accessed May 30, 2020).

Exstein, Ted. "What is the difference between the Talmud and the Torah?" *Quora.* July 16, 2015. https://www.quora.com/What-is-the-difference-between-the-Talmud-and-the-Torah (accessed October 15, 2018).

Fackenheim, Emil L. "Judaism & the Meaning of Life." *Commentary.* April 1, 1965. https://www.commentarymagazine.com/articles/judaism-the-meaning-of-life/ (accessed March 27, 2018).

Feddacheenee. "File:Annunciator.jpg." *Wikimedia Commons.* June 29, 2012. https://commons.wikimedia.org/wiki/File:Annunciator.jpg (accessed June 16, 2019).

Finkelstein, J. "File:Maslow's hierarchy of needs.svg." *Wikimedia Commons.* October 27, 2006. https://commons.wikimedia.org/wiki/File:Maslow%27s_hierarchy_of_needs.svg (accessed June 14, 2019).

Fish, Stanley. *Winning Arguments, What works and Doesn't Work in Politics, The Bedroom, The Curtroom, and the Classroom.* New York: Harper Collins, 2016.

Foner, Eric. "The Corrupt Bargain." *London Review of Books.* May 221, 2020. https://www.lrb.co.uk/the-paper/v42/n10/eric-foner/the-corrupt-bargain?utm_campaign=wp_todays_worldview&utm_medium=email&utm_source=newsletter&wpisrc=nl_todayworld (accessed May 15, 2020).

Frea, Dick. "SS Jerimiah O'Brien." *National Park Service - WWII In the San Francisco Bay Area.* n.d. https://www.nps.gov/nr/travel/wwiibayarea/jer.HTM (accessed June 16, 2019).

Frederick Clarkson - Project Blitz by Any Other Name. "Project Blitz by Any Other Name." *Political Research Associates.* Nov 7, 2019. https://www.politicalresearch.org/2019/11/07/project-blitz-any-other-name (accessed May 28, 2020).

Freeman, James Dill. *The Household of Faith, Chapter XI, "Their Healing Work, "Heal the Sick" "".* 1951. https://www.truthunity.net/books/the-household-of-faith-155-164 (accessed January 25, 2018).

Fritz, Robert. *Corporate Tides.* Oxford, England: Butterworth-Hinemann, 1994.

—. *Creating.* New York: Fawcett Columbine, 1991.

—. *The Leader as Creator.* Salem, Massachusetts: DMA, 1986.

—. *The Path of Least Resistance - Learning to Become the Creative Force in Your Own Life.* New York: Fawcett Columbine, 1989.

—. *The Path of Least Resistance for Managers - Designing Organizations to Succeed.* San Francisco: Berret-Koehler Publishers, 1999.

Funk, Ken. "Perspectives on Science and Christian Faith." *American Scientific Affiliation.* September 2007. http://www.asa3.org/ASA/PSCF/2007/PSCF9-07Funk.pdf (accessed March 7, 2018).

Gaylor, Annie Laurie. "Freethought of the Day." *Freedom From Religion Foundation.* Edited by Annie Laurie Gaylor. February 15, 2017. https://ffrf.org/news/day (accessed February 15, 2017).

Giovannoli, Joseph. *The Biology of Belief - How Our Biology Biases Our Beliefs and Perceptions.* Rosetta Press, Inc, 2000.

Goldhill, Olivia. "The person who's best at lying to you is you." *Quartz.* March 18, 2018. https://qz.com/1231534/the-person-whos-best-at-lying-to-you-is-you/ (accessed March 19, 2018).

Gray, Jason D. "Buddhist Views of the Afterlife." *The Immortality Project, University of California, Riverside.* n.d. http://www.sptimmortalityproject.com/background/buddhist-views-of-the-afterlife/ (accessed March 2, 2018).

Green, Khalil. "Love for God in Islam - The Highest Attribute of Spiritual Attainment." *IslamiCity*. March 15, 2015. http://www.islamicity.org/6526/love-for-god-in-islam-the-highest-attribute-of-spiritual-attainment/ (accessed March 1, 2018).

Gregorie, Rev. John. "Nazarene Lord's Prayer." *The Tau*. n.d. https://sites.google.com/site/thetaugbbo00/nazarene-lord-s-prayer (accessed April 12, 2019).

Grew, David. *Paddy Points the Way*. New York: Coward-McCann, 1950.

Guareschi, Giovannino. *The Little World of Don Camilo*. New York: Pellegrini and Cudahy, 1950.

Gunasekara, Dr V. A. "The Buddhist Attitude to God." *BuddhaSasana*. April 1997. https://www.budsas.org/ebud/ebdha068.htm (accessed February 26, 2018).

Guthrie, Woody. "This Land Is Your Land." *Woody Guthrie*. 1956 (renewed), 1958 (renewed), 1970, and 1972. https://www.woodyguthrie.org/Lyrics/This_Land.htm (accessed May 2, 2020).

Hafner, Katie - As Catholic Hospitals Expand, So Do Limits on Some Procedures. "As Catholic Hospitals Expand, So Do Limits on Some Procedures." *New York Time*. Aug 10, 2018r. https://www.nytimes.com/2018/08/10/health/catholic-hospitals-procedures.html (accessed May 1, 2020).

Hall, Douglas John. *God & Human Suffering*. Minneapollis: Augsburg Publishing House, 1986.

Hanh, Thich Nhat. "Buddhist Quotes." *The Buddhist Center*. n.d. http://www.thebuddhacenter.org/buddhism/buddhist-quotes/ (accessed March 20, 2018).

Hare, John Bruno. "Hinduism." *Internet Sacred Text Archive*. 2010. http://www.sacred-texts.com/hin/ (accessed October 17, 2018).

Harwell, Jaclyn. "Why Joy is More Important to Your Health than Food." *The Family That Heals Together*. May 22, 2016. https://www.thefamilythathealstogether.com/joy-important-health-food/ (accessed February 8, 2018).

"Having Hope in Allah The Almighty - I." *Islamweb.net English*. August 10, 2015. http://www.islamweb.net/en/article/178489/having-hope-in-allah-the-almighty-i (accessed March 20, 2019).

Hawkes, Brent. "Spirituality and sexuality. You can have both." *TEDxToronto*. December 7, 2015. https://www.youtube.com/watch?v=7NGB5rQKkpM (accessed December 20, 2018).

HealthCare Chaplaincy . ""Handbook of Patients' Spiritual and Cultural Values for Health Care Professionals" -Finding Meaning – Bringing Comfort." *healthcarechaplaincy.org*. 2013. http://www.healthcarechaplaincy.org/userimages/Cultural%20Sensitivity%20handbook%20from%20HealthCare%20Chaplaincy%20%20(3-12%202013).pdf (accessed November 6, 2018).

Herbert J. Gans, The Nation - This Is How the Republican Party Plans to Destroy the Federal Government. "This Is How the Republican Party Plans to Destroy the Federal Government." *The Nation*. Feb 13, 2017. https://www.thenation.com/article/archive/this-is-how-the-republican-party-plans-to-destroy-the-federal-government/ (accessed May 30, 2020).

Hess, Abigail. "Here's how much the average student loan borrower owes when they graduate." *CNBC.com*. May 20, 2019. https://www.cnbc.com/2019/05/20/how-much-the-average-student-loan-borrower-owes-when-they-graduate.html (accessed May 4, 2020).

Hill, Napoleon. *Think and Grow Rich*. n.d.

Himilayan Academy, Saiva Siddhanta Theological Seminary at Kauai's Hindu Monastery. "Karma and Reincarnation." *Himilayanacademy.com*. n.d. https://www.himalayanacademy.com/readlearn/basics/karma-reincarnation (accessed March 21, 2018).

—. "TEACH HOW HINDUISM GRANTS EXPERIENCE OF GOD." *Raising Children As Good Hindus*. n.d. https://www.himalayanacademy.com/media/books/raising-children-as-good-hindus_ei/web/ch37_sec6.html (accessed March 1, 2018).

Hindu, The. "Experiencing God ." *The Hindu*. October 28, 2016. http://www.the-hindu.com/features/friday-review/religion/Experiencing-God/article12543677.ece (accessed March 1, 2018).

Hindupedia. "Ideals and Values/Forgiveness." *Hindupedia*. n.d. http://www.hindupedia.com/en/Ideals_and_Values/Forgiveness (accessed February 19, 2018).

—. "Nature of God (This article was originally published in the April/May/June 2009 edition of "Hinduism Today"." *Hindupedia*. April 2009. http://www.hindupedia.com/en/Who_is_a_Hindu%3F#The_Nature_of_God (accessed Februry 27, 2018).

History - Great Depression History. "Great Depression History." *History.com*. n.d. https://www.history.com/topics/great-depression/great-depression-history (accessed May 7, 2020).

History - Labor Movement. "Labor Movement." *History.com*. Mar 31, 2020. https://www.history.com/topics/19th-century/labor (accessed May 6, 2020).

History.com Editors - 18th and 21st Amendments . "18th and 21st Amendments ." *History*. Jan 6, 2020. https://www.history.com/topics/united-states-constitution/18th-and-21st-amendments (accessed May 8, 2020).

History.com Editors - Scopes Trial. "Scopes Trial." *History*. Jun 10, 2019. https://www.history.com/topics/roaring-twenties/scopes-trial (accessed May 8, 2020).

Hitchens, Christofer. *the Portable Atheist*. Philadelphia: Da Capo OPress, a member of th Perseus Books Group, 2007.

Hitchens, Christopher. "4 Clips of Our Greatly Missed Hitch." *Youyube*. n.d. https://www.youtube.com/watch?v=HKRonSOYBN8 (accessed October 4, 2018).

Horodysky, Daniel. "American Mariners in World War II: First to Go; Last to Return." *Berkeley Daily Planet*. December 6, 1999. http://www.usmm.org/pearl-harbor.html (accessed April 13, 2019).

Housing Wire - Republicans move to abolish CFPB. "Republicans move to abolish CFPB." *Housing Wirre*. May 7, 2019. https://www.housingwire.com/articles/48980-republicans-move-to-abolish-cfpb/ (accessed May 30, 2020).

Intelligent Design - What is Intelligent Design? "What Is Intelligent Design? ." *https://intelligentdesign.org/*. n.d. https://intelligentdesign.org/whatisid/ (accessed May 8, 2020).

International Planetarium Society, Incorporated. "The Age of the Earth and the Universe." n.d. http://www.ips-planetarium.org/?age (accessed November 12, 2016).

Izquierdo, German. "What is the purpose of life according to Judaism?" *Quora*. January 19, 2017. https://www.quora.com/What-is-the-purpose-of-life-according-to-Judaism (accessed March 27, 2018).

Jacoby, Susan. *Freethinkers*. New York : Metropolitan/Owl Book, Henry Holt and Company, 2004.

jannah.org. "The Attributes of God." *Islam 101*. February 26, 2018. http://www.islam101.com/tauheed/AllahNames.htm (accessed February 26, 2018).

Jason Plautz - How to Eliminate Almost Every Federal Agency. "How to Eliminate Almost Every Federal Agency." *The Atlantic*. Aug 13, 2014. https://www.theatlantic.com/politics/archive/2014/08/how-to-eliminate-almost-every-federal-agency/452961/ (accessed May 19, 2020).

Jennifer Rubin - Washington Post - George H.W. Bush and the 'L' word. "George H.W. Bush and the 'L' word." *Washington Post*. Dec 3, 2018. https://www.washingtonpost.com/news/opinions/wp/2018/12/03/george-h-w-bush-and-the-l-word/ (accessed Ma7 31, 2020).

Jerry Bergman - Answers In Genesis - Darwinism and the Nazi Race Holocaust. "Darwinism and the Nazi Race Holocaust." *Answers In Genesis*. Nov 1, 1999. https://answersingenesis.org/charles-darwin/racism/darwinism-and-the-nazi-race-holocaust/ (accessed May 8, 2020).

John Gramlich - Pew Research Center - What the data says about gun deaths in the U.S. "What the data says about gun deaths in the U.S." *Pew Research Center - Factank News in Numbers*. Aug 19, 2019. https://www.pewresearch.org/fact-tank/2019/08/16/what-the-data-says-about-gun-deaths-in-the-u-s/ (accessed May 26, 2020).

Jones, Robert. *The End of White Christian America*. New York: Simon & Schuster, 2016.

Judiasm 101. n.d. http://www.jewfaq.org/613.htm (accessed November 6, 2017).

Kandell, Ellen. "Objectivity, Subjectivity, and the Known Unknows: Intentions vs. Assumptions in Conflict Resolution." *Alternative Resolutions*. June 3, 2016. https://www.alternativeresolutions.net/2016/06/03/intentions-vs-assumptions/ (accessed June 16, 2019).

Karmapa, His Holiness the Gyalwang Karmapa. "Love and Compassion: Transforming our Relationships for the Better." *The Karmapa*. June 23, 2016. http://kagyuoffice.org/love-and-compassion-transforming-our-relationships-for-the-better/ (accessed February 16, 2019).

Keller, Timothy. *Making Sense of GOD - An Invitation tothe Skeptical*. New York: Penguin Random House LL, 375 Hudson Street, New York, 2016.

Khandavalli, Shankara Bharadwaj. "Karma." *Hindupedia*. n.d. http://www.hindupedia.com/en/Karma (accessed March 2, 2018).

Kivata. "What, according to Hinduism, is the purpose of life?" *Quroa*. December 16, 2016. https://www.quora.com/What-according-to-Hinduism-is-the-purpose-of-life (accessed March 27, 2018).

Koch, Richard. *The 80/20 Principle: The Secret to Achieving More with Less*. New York: Currency Doubleday, 1998.

Kornfield, Jack. "Why Practice it? (Forgiveness)." *Greater Good Magazine - Science Based Insights for a Meaningful Life*. n.d. https://greatergood.berkeley.edu/topic/forgiveness/definition#why-practice (accessed October 4, 2018).

Krista Niles. "ERA." *ERA*. Jan 27, 2020. https://www.equalrightsamendment.org/blog/2020/1/27/x0pqlkthiacyhpt31lxbppxthnxh6d (accessed May 5, 2020).

Kruger, J, and Dunning. D. "Unskilled and unaware of it: How difficulties in recognizing one's own incompetence lead to inflated self-assessments." *Journal of Personality and Social Psychology, 77(6), 1121-1134.* . Dec 1999. http://psycnet.apa.org/doiLanding?doi=10.1037%2F0022-3514.77.6.1121 (accessed March 19, 2018).

Kukkonen, Tuuli. "Still Going Strong: Sexuality in Older Adults." *TEDxGuelphU*. March 17, 2017. https://www.youtube.com/watch?v=pqLhP-POEJB4 (accessed December 19, 2018).

Kumar, Anjali. "My failed mission to find God — and what I found instead ." *Ted Talks Worth Spreading*. January 2018. https://www.ted.com/speakers/anjali_kumar (accessed February 1, 2018).

Lambert, Malcolm. *God's Armies - Crusade and Jihad: Origins, History, Aftermath*. New York London: Pegasus Books, 2016.

Lascola, Linda. "Our True Religion: Football, Firearms, and the American Flag." *Patheos - Nonreligious*. November 8, 2018. https://www.patheos.com/blogs/rationaldoubt/2018/11/our-true-religion-football-firearms-and-the-american-flag/?utm_medium=email&utm_source=BRSS&utm_campaign=Nonreligious&utm_content=456 (accessed November 8, 2018).

Lee Fang - The Intercept - Foreign-Funded Dark-Money Groups Lobby IRS to Repeal Remaining Reporting Requirements. "Foreign-Funded Dark-Money Groups Lobby IRS to Repeal Remaining Reporting Requirements." *The Intercept*. Feb 15, 2020. https://theintercept.com/2020/02/15/dark-money-irs-reporting-501c/ (accessed May 30, 2020).

Leitch, Cliff. "What Does the Bible Say About Love?" *The Christian Bible Reference Site*. January 1, 2010. http://www.christianbiblereference.org/faq_love.htm (accessed February 12, 2018).

—. "What Does the Bible Say About the Old Testament Law?" *Christian Bible Reference Site*. 1996-2014. http://www.christianbiblereference.org/faq_OldTestamentLaw.htm (accessed February 2, 2018).

Lewis, C.S. *Mere Christianity*. New York: Harper Collins, 2004.

Linder, Doug. "Bishop James Ussher Sets the Date for Creation." 2004. http://law2.umkc.edu/faculty/projects/ftrials/scopes/ussher.html (accessed November 12, 2016).

Lisa Rein & Damian Palleta, Washington Post - If Trump has his way, this major federal agency is on the way out. "If Trump has his way, this major federal agency is on the way out." *Washington Post*. Apr 10, 2019. https://www.washingtonpost.com/politics/if-trump-has-his-way-this-major-federal-agency-is-on-the-way-out/2019/04/09/935e2dfe-54c0-11e9-9136-f8e636f1f6df_story.html (accessed Apr 30, 2020).

Livni, Ephrat. "A Nobel Prize-winning psychologist says most people don't really want to be happy." *Quartz - #Lifegoals*. December 21, 2018. https://qz.com/1503207/a-nobel-prize-winning-psychologist-defines-happiness-versus-satisfaction/ (accessed December 21, 2018).

Lombard, Jay Dr. *The Mind of God - Neuroscience, Faith, and a Search for the Soul*. New York: Crown Publishing Group, a divisioin of Pengin Random House LLC, 2017.

Longenecker, Dwight. "Why Does God Allow Horrible Evil?" *National Catholic Register*. February 23, 2017. http://www.ncregister.com/blog/longenecker/why-does-god-allow-horrible-evil (accessed February 28, 2017).

Lumen Learning. "Introduction to Psychology - Humanistic Approaches." *Lumen Learning Courses*. n.d. https://courses.lumenlearning.com/waymaker-psychology/chapter/humanistic-approaches/ (accessed February 8, 2019).

Luskin, Fred. "What is Forgiveness?" *Greater Good Magazine - Science Based Insights for a Meaningful Life*. n.d. https://greatergood.berkeley.edu/topic/forgiveness/definition (accessed October 4, 2018).

Lyle, Kevin. "Helicopter Royal Air Force." *Pixabay.com*. May 26, 2014. https://pixabay.com/photos/helicopter-royal-air-force-chinook-354699/ (accessed June 16, 2019).

—. "kvnlyle." *Pixabay*. May 26, 2014. https://pixabay.com/photos/helicopter-royal-air-force-chinook-354699/ (accessed June 16, 2019).

Macrotrends. "Germany Population Growth Rate 1950-2020." *macrotrends*. 2020. https://www.macrotrends.net/countries/DEU/germany/population-growth-rate (accessed May 1, 2020).

"Making myths out of the Titanic (From Book, Titanic Lives, by Richard-Davenport Hines, Harper Press)." *Church Times*. April 11, 2012 (Picture taken on Titanic 1912). https://www.churchtimes.co.uk/articles/2012/13-april/comment/making-myths-out-of-the-titanic (accessed August 3, 2019).

Malaekah, Mostafa. "What is the Purpose of Life?" *islam-guide.com*. 2001. https://www.islam-guide.com/purpose-of-life.htm#s8 (accessed March 27, 2018).

Maltz, Maxwell. *Psycho-Cybernetics*. New York: Pocket Books a division of Simon & Schuster, 1989.

Manson, Mark. *The Subtle Art of Not Giving a F*ck*. New York: Harper One, 2016.

Marc Zvi Brettler, Peter Enns, Daniel J. Harrington. *The Bible and the Believer*. New York: Oxford University Press, 2012.

Mark Hertling, Lieutant General - Obesity is a National Security Issue. "Obesity is a National Security Issue." *YouTube TEDxMidAtlantic*. 2012. https://www.youtube.com/watch?v=sWN13pKVp9s (accessed May 25, 2020).

Maroof, Rabbi Joseph Maroof. "What does Judaism Say About Love." *Ask the Rabiis*. September/October 2010. Rabbi Joseph Maroof (accessed February 13, 2018).

Maroof, Rabbi Joseph. "What Does Judaism Say About Love pg 25." *Ask the Rabbis*. September-October 2010. http://www.momentmag.com/wp-content/uploads/2013/02/What-Does-Judaism-Say-About-Love.pdf (accessed February 13, 2018).

Martha F. Davis - American Constitution Society - To Promote the General Welfare. "To Promote the General Welfare." *American Constitution Society.* Sep 15, 2011. https://www.acslaw.org/expertforum/to-promote-the-general-welfare/ (accessed May 28, 2020).

Matthew Flemming, Roll Call - The 5 Agencies Ted Cruz Would Cut. "The 5 Agencies Ted Cruz Would Cut." *Roll Call.* Nov 11, 2015. https://www.rollcall.com/2015/11/11/the-5-agencies-ted-cruz-would-cut/ (accessed May 30, 2020).

McCandless, Jeremy R. "Experiencing God - Day By Day." *Books.Google.com.* 2012. https://books.google.com/books?isbn=1471637093 (accessed March 1, 2018).

McCoy, Maxie. "Are you sabotaging everything you want? How to know." *Ladders.* March 7, 2019. https://www.theladders.com/career-advice/are-you-sabotaging-everything-you-want-how-to-know (accessed March 7, 2019).

McGrath, James F. "Naming the Animals, Young-Earth Creationist Style." *Patheos - Progressive Christiain.* October 12, 2018. http://www.patheos.com/blogs/religionprof/2018/10/naming-the-animals-young-earth-creationist-style.html?utm_source=Newsletter&utm_medium=email&utm_campaign=Progressive+Christian&utm_content=43 (accessed October 12, 2018).

McGrath, Maureen. "No Sex Marriage – Masturbation, Loneliness, Cheating and Shame." *TEDxStanleyPark.* July 6, 2016. https://www.youtube.com/watch?v=LVgzOyHVcj4&t=206s (accessed December 20, 2018).

—. "No Sex Marriage – Masturbation, Loneliness, Cheating and Shame." *TEDxStanleyPark.* July 6, 2016. https://www.youtube.com/watch?v=LVgzOyHVcj4 (accessed June 20, 2019).

McLeod, Ken. "Forgiveness Is Not Buddhist." *Tricycle.* 2017. https://tricycle.org/magazine/forgiveness-not-buddhist/ (accessed February 19, 2018).

Melanie Warner - Machine Politics In the Digital Age. "Machine Politics In the Digital Age." *New York Times.* Nov 9, 2003. https://www.nytimes.com/2003/11/09/business/machine-politics-in-the-digital-age.html (accessed May 22, 2020).

Merritt, Carol Howard. *Healing Spiritual Wounds.* New York, New York: HarperOne, 2017.

Meslier, Jean. "Superstition In All Ages (1732)." *Gutenburg.org.* January 25, 2013. https://www.gutenberg.org/files/17607/17607-h/17607-h.htm#link2H_4_0013 (accessed March 23, 2018).

Meyers, Pamela. "How to spot a liar." *TED Global 2011.* October 11, 2011. https://www.youtube.com/watch?v=P_6vDLq64gE (accessed September 15, 2018).

Michael P. McDonald - National Election Project. "National General Election VEP Turnout Rates, 1789-Present." *National Election Project.* n.d. http://www.electproject.org/national-1789-present (accessed May 22, 2020).

Miles, Charles A. "In the Garden." *Timeless Truths.* 1913. http://library.timelesstruths.org/music/In_the_Garden/ https://creativecommons.org/licenses/by-sa/3.0/ (accessed November 6, 2016).

Military Uniform Supply Company. "Genuine Vietnam-Era OG-107 Boonie Hat with Insect Net." *Military Clothing.com.* n.d. https://www. militaryclothing.com/Genuine-Vietnam-Era-OG-107-Boonie-Hat-with-Insect-Net.aspx?id=19818-60002-ABM-6&gclid=CjwKCAjwq-TmBRBdEi-wAaO1enxH2qTnSAUwYdvXyRwa-XZYngKFu5FiHoipYZfTa4qNffFUgk-BOD1hoCZYYQAvD_BwE (accessed May 15, 2019).

MJL Staff. "Hatikvah, the National Anthem of Israel." *My Jewish Learning.* n.d. https://www.myjewishlearning.com/article/national-anthem-of-israel/ (accessed March 20, 2018).

—. "Is There A Jewish Afterlife?" *My Jewish Learning.* n.d. https://www.myjewishle-arning.com/article/life-after-death/ (accessed March 2, 2018).

—. "Jewish Resurrection of the Dead." *My Jewish Larning.* n.d. https://www.myjew-ishlearning.com/article/jewish-resurrection-of-the-dead/ (accessed March 2, 2018).

—. "Judaism and Sex: Questions and Answers." *My Jewish Learning.* 2018. https:// www.myjewishlearning.com/article/judaism-and-sex-questions-and-answers/ (accessed February 10, 2018).

—. "Tzitzit, the Fringes on the Prayer Shawl." *My Jewish Learning.* 2018. https://www. myjewishlearning.com/article/tzitzit/ (accessed February 10, 2018).

Mooney, Chris. *The REPUBLICAN WAR on SCIENCE.* New York: Basic Books, 2005.

Moran, Mark CEO. "Buddhist Sacred Texts: The Sutras." *Finding Dulcinea.* 2018? http://www.findingdulcinea.com/guides/Religion-and-Spirituality/Sa-cred-Texts.xa_1.html (accessed March 13, 2018).

—. "Hinduism: Understanding Sanatana Dharma." *Finding Dulcinea.* n.d. http://www. findingdulcinea.com/guides/Religion-and-Spirituality/Hinduism.pg_0.html#0 (accessed March 13, 2018).

Morehouse, Andrew R. *Voltaire and Jean Meslier.* New Haven: Yale University Press, 1936.

Moultman, Jurgend. "Theology of Hope by Jurgen Moltmann." *On-line JournL OF Public Theology.* n.d. http://www.pubtheo.com/theologians/moltmann/theolo-gy-of-hope-0b.htm (accessed March 19, 2018).

Muller, Richard A. *Now - The Physics of Time.* New York: W.W Norton & Company, 2016.

Murakami, Haruki. "Thailand." *Granta - The Magazine of New Writing.* 2011. https:// granta.com/thailand/ (accessed February 8, 2019).

Murray, David. "8 Sources of Joy vs. 6 Thieves of It." *Christianity.com.* n.d. https:// www.christianity.com/blogs/david-murray/8-sources-of-joy-vs-6-thieves-of-it. html (accessed March 22, 2018).

Nachman, Rabbi. "Experiencing the Presence of God." *JewishOutlook.com.* 2014. http://jewishoutlook.com/experiencing-the-presence-of-god/ (accessed March 1, 2018).

Naomi Jagoda - Senate Republicans reintroduce bill to repeal the estate tax. "Senate Republicans reintroduce bill to repeal the estate tax." *The Hill.* Jan 28, 2019. https://thehill.com/policy/finance/427328-senate-republicans-reintro-duce-bill-to-repeal-the-estate-tax (accessed May 19, 2020).

Neil, Herms. "Erika." *Wikipedia.* 1930's. https://en.wikipedia.org/wiki/Erika_(song) (accessed January 22, 2017).

Newlyn, Emma. "Ganesh: The mudra, the meaning and the story of the elephant-headed god." *Yoga Matters.* March 6, 2017. https://www.yogamatters.com/blog/ganesh-mudra-meaning-story-elephant-headed-god/ (accessed October 8, 2018).

Nichols, Tom. "How America Lost Faith in Expertise (And Why Tgat's a Giant Problem)." *Foreign Affairs*, March/April 2017: 60-73.

NOLAN D. MCCASKILL and MATTHEW NUSSBAUM - Trump signs executive order requiring that for every one new regulation, two must be revoked. "Trump signs executive order requiring that for every one new regulation, two must be revoked." *Politico.* Jan 17, 2017. https://www.politico.com/story/2017/01/trump-signs-executive-order-requiring-that-for-every-one-new-regulation-two-must-be-revoked-234365 (accessed May 19, 2020).

Novella, Steven. *Skptic's Guide to the Universe.* New York: Grand Central Publishing, 2018.

NPR - When Did Companies Become People? "When Did Companies Become People? Excavating The Legal Evolution." *NPR.org - Law.* Jul 28, 2014. https://www.npr.org/2014/07/28/335288388/when-did-companies-become-people-excavating-the-legal-evolution (accessed May 4, 2020).

Numrich, Paul. "Flow Chart of a Religous Ethical System." Self Published Paper, July 2018.

Nunez, Paul L. *The New Science of Consciousness - Exploring the Complexity of Brain, Mind, and Self.* Amerhest, New Yor: Prometheus Books, 2016.

Olivia, Keeley. "Masturbation is the New Meditation." *TEDxLeamingtonSpa.* November 28, 2018. https://www.youtube.com/watch?v=BUOzUTXFlQA&t=8s (accessed December 12, 2018).

O'Neill, Tim. "Jesus the Apocalyptic Prophet." *History for Atheists.* December 20, 2018. https://historyforatheists.com/2018/12/jesus-apocalyptic-prophet/ (accessed April 13, 2019).

OpenSecrets - What is a PAC? "What is a PAC?" *OpenSecrets.org.* n.d. https://www.opensecrets.org/pacs/pacfaq.php (accessed May 4, 2020).

Oshin, Mayo. "10 lessons from Benjamin Franklin's daily schedule that will double your productivity." *Ladders - Productivity.* February 11, 2019. 10 lessons from Benjamin Franklin's daily schedule that will double your productivity (accessed February 11, 2019).

—. "The Iron Mike rule: The one thing successful people do differently." *Ladders.* November 26, 2018. https://www.theladders.com/career-advice/the-iron-mike-rule-the-one-thing-successful-people-do-differently (accessed November 26, 2018).

OSIA - Italian Americans in the US. "Italian Americans in the US." *OSIA.* 2004. https://www.osia.org/wp-content/uploads/2017/05/IA_Profile.pdf (accessed May 18, 2020).

Patrick Malone & R. Jeffry Smith - GOP chair of nuclear safety agency secretly urges Trump to abolish it . "GOP chair of nuclear safety agency secretly urges Trump to abolish it ." *Center for Public Integrity.* Feb 7, 2018. https://publicintegrity.org/national-security/gop-chair-of-nuclear-safety-agency-secretly-urges-trump-to-abolish-it/ (accessed May 30, 2020).

Paul Fidalgo - Center for Inquiry - Eugenie Scott and Bertha Vazquez on "Reaching the 60%" for Evolution Education. "Eugenie Scott and Bertha Vazquez on "Reaching the 60%" for Evolution Education." *Center for Inquiry.* Oct 29, 2016. https://centerforinquiry.org/blog/eugenie-scott-and-bertha-vasquez-on-reaching-the-60-for-evolution-education/ (accessed May 8, 2020).

Payne, Richard. "The Authority of the Buddha: ." *Institute of Buddhist Studies, 2140 Durant Avenue, Berkeley CA 94704, U.S.A.* n.d. http://www.zurnalai.vu.lt/acta-orientalia-vilnensia/article/viewFile/3660/5149 (accessed March 7, 018).

Peter Defazio - US Congressman. "DeFazio-Authored Bill to Help US Postal Service Maintain Sustainability ." *Peter Defazio - US Congressman.* Feb 5, 2020. https://defazio.house.gov/media-center/press-releases/defazio-authored-bill-to-help-us-postal-service-maintain-sustainability (accessed May 22, 2020).

Peter G. Peterson Foundation - How Does the U.S. Healthcare System Compare to Other Countries? "How Does the U.S. Healthcare System Compare to Other Countries?" *Peter G. Peterson Foundation.* Jul 22, 2019. https://www.pgpf.org/blog/2019/07/how-does-the-us-healthcare-system-compare-to-other-countries (accessed May 25, 2020).

Peter G. Peterson Foundation - U.S. Defense Spending Compared to Other Countries . "U.S. Defense Spending Compared to Other Countries ." *Peter G. Peterson Foundation.* May 13, 2020. https://www.pgpf.org/chart-archive/0053_defense-comparison (accessed May 25, 2020).

Peterson, Kay, and David A. Kolb. *How You Learn is How You LIve.* Oakland, California: Berrett_Koehler Publishers, Inc, 2017.

Peto, Alan. "Buddhism for Beginners (a Quick Intro)." *Alan Peto.* December 14, 2011. https://www.alanpeto.com/buddhism/buddhism-quick-intro/ (accessed October 22, 2018).

Pew Research Center - Jynnah Radford. "Key findings about U.S. immigrants." *Pew Research Center.* Jun 17, 2019. https://www.pewresearch.org/fact-tank/2019/06/17/key-findings-about-u-s-immigrants/ (accessed May 1, 2020).

Pilgrim, Peace (aka Mildred Lisette Norman). *Peace Pilgrim Her Life and Work In Her Own Words.* Sante Fe, New Mexico, USA: Ocean Tree Books, 1983.

Piper, John. "What Is So Important About Christian Hope? ." *desiring God.* March 7, 2008. https://www.desiringgod.org/interviews/what-is-so-important-about-christian-hope (accessed March 20, 2018).

Pope, Msg Charles. "The Church Cannot Teach Error, Because She Was Founded by Jesus Christ, Who is God Himself." *National Catholic Register.* February 21, 2017. http://www.ncregister.com/blog/msgr-pope/the-church-cannot-teach-error-because-she-was-founded-by-jesus-christ-who-i (accessed February 28, 2017).

Prabhupada, Bhaktivedanta Swami. *Bhagavad-Gita - As it is*. Australia: McPherson's Printing Group, 2001.

Pratt, Ralph S. "I Was There! - I Was on the Bombed Steel Seafarer." *The War Illustrated*. September 30, 1941. I Was There! - I Was on the Bombed Steel Seafarer (accessed April 13, 2019).

"Pratyahara (Con't) – The Sense Organs." *Discover-yoga-online.com*. n.d. http://www. discover-yoga-online.com/sense-organs.html (accessed April 11, 2019).

Prothero, Stephen. *Religious Literacy - What every American Needs to Know - and Doesn't*. New York: Harper One - Harper Collins, 2008.

"Quotations on: Joy, Happiness ." *A View on Buddhism*. n.d. http://viewonbuddhism. org/dharma-quotes-quotations-buddhist/joy-happiness.htm (accessed March 26, 2018).

Rabbi. "Temple Ner Ami." *http://templenerami.org/*. November 2006. templenerami. org/.../Old/Nov%2006%20Good%20Evil%20and%20Freewill.pdf (accessed February 8, 2018).

Rasheta, Noah. "27 – Understanding Non-Attachment." *Secular Buddhism*. September 19, 2016. https://secularbuddhism.com/understanding-non-attachment/ (accessed October 31, 2018).

Raven. "File:Flammarion-color.png." *Wikimedia*. March 15, 2015. https://commons. wikimedia.org/w/index.php?curid=39827732 (accessed Auguest 1, 2019).

Reinke, Tony. *12 Ways Your Phone is Changing You*. Wheaton, Illinois: Crossway, 2017.

Rich, Tracey R. "Beliefs." *Judaism 101*. 2011. http://www.jewfaq.org/defs/beliefs.htm (accessed March 13, 2018).

—. "Halakhah: Jewish Law." *Judaism 101*. 2011. http://www.jewfaq.org/halakhah.htm (accessed March 13, 2018).

—. "The Nature of G-d." *Judaism 101*. 2011. http://www.jewfaq.org/g-d.htm (accessed February 26, 2018).

—. "What Do Jews Believe?" *Judaism 101*. 2011. http://www.jewfaq.org/beliefs.htm (accessed March 18, 2018).

Rich, Tracy R. "Love and Brotherhood." *Judaism 101*. 1995-201). http://www.jewfaq. org/brother.htm (accessed February 13, 2018).

Richard W. Hatcher III - South Carolina Encyclopedia - "States Rights Gist". "Gist, States Rights." *South Carolina Encyclopedia*. Aug 10, 2016. http://www.scencyclo- pedia.org/sce/entries/gist-states-rights/ (accessed May 27, 2020).

Rizvi, Sayyid Muhammad Rizvi. "Chapter Two: The Islamic Sexual Morality (1) Its Foundation." *Al-Islam.org*. Islamic Education & Information Center. 2018. https://www.al-islam.org/marriage-and-morals-islam-sayyid-muhammad-rizvi/ chapter-two-islamic-sexual-morality-1-its-foundation (accessed February 10, 2018).

Robin. "The Buddhist Outlook on Hope." *Buddhist Teachings*. April 16, 2013. http:// www.buddhistteachings.org/the-buddhist-outlook-on-hope (accessed Novem- ber 19, 2018).

Roosevelt, Franklin. "On Maintaining Freedom of the Sea." *FDR Library*. Septem- ber 11, 1941. http://docs.fdrlibrary.marist.edu/091141.html (accessed April 13, 2019).

S., Pangambam. "Maureen McGrath: No Sex Marriage – Masturbation, Loneliness, Cheating and Shame (Transcript)." *The Singju Post*. September 2, 2016. https://singjupost.com/maureen-mcgrath-no-sex-marriage-masturbation-loneliness-cheating-and-shame-transcript/3/ (accessed June 20, 2019).

Sacks, Jonathan Rabbi. "Faith Lectures: Judaism, Justice and Tragedy – Confronting the problem of evil." *http://rabbisacks.org/*. April 6, 2000. http://rabbisacks.org/faith-lectures-judaism-justice-and-tragedy-confronting-the-problem-of-evil/ (accessed February 8, 2018).

—. "Future Tense – How The Jews Invented Hope." *Rabbi Sachs*. April 1, 2008. http://rabbisacks.org/future-tense-how-the-jews-invented-hope-published-in-the-jewish-chronicle/ (accessed 2018 20, March).

—. "The Pursuit of Joy." *Orthodox Union*. n.d. https://www.ou.org/torah/parsha/rabbi-sacks-on-parsha/the-pursuit-of-joy/ (accessed March 26, 2018).

Sallman, Warner. "Christ at Heart's Door." *The Warner Sallman Collection*. 1942. http://www.warnersallman.com/collection/images/christ-at-hearts-door/ (accessed November 6, 2016).

Sarah O'Brien - CNBC - Companies get to defer payroll tax payments. "Companies get to defer payroll tax payments under coronavirus relief bill. Here's what that means for workers." *CNBC*. May 25, 2020. https://www.cnbc.com/2020/03/25/companies-may-get-payroll-tax-relief-under-coronavirus-stimulus-bill.html (accessed May 28, 2020).

Sarah Pruitt - George Washington Warned Against Political Infighting in His Farewell Address. "George Washington Warned Against Political Infighting in His Farewell Address." *Hisory*. Feb 18, 2020. https://www.history.com/news/george-washington-farewell-address-warnings (accessed May 25, 2020).

Satlow, Michael. "How the Bible Became Holy." *ReformJudaism.org*. n.d. https://reformjudaism.org/jewish-life/arts-culture/literature/how-bible-became-holy (accessed March 7, 2018).

Schwartz, Gary E. PhD. *The Aferlife Experiments*. New York, NY: Atria Books, 2002.

Seidel, Andrew L. - The Founding Myth. *The Founding Myth*. New York: Sterling, 2019.

Shade, Leah D. "I Want Jesus to Let Me Off the Hook: The Rich Young Man and Me." *Patheos - Eco Preacher*. October 10, 2018. http://www.patheos.com/blogs/ecopreacher/2018/10/jesus-hook-rich-young-man-me/?utm_source=Newsletter&utm_medium=email&utm_campaign=Progressive+Christian&utm_content=43 (accessed October 12, 2018).

Shah, Zia, H. "Two Hundred Verses about Compassionate Living in the Quran." *The Muslim Times* . October 29, 2013. https://themuslimtimes.info/2013/10/29/three-hundred-verses-about-compassionate-living-in-the-quran/ (accessed February 15, 2018).

Shakir, M.H. *The Qur'an*. Elmhurst, New York: Tahrike Tarsile Qur'an, Inc., 2004 9th U.S. Edition.

Shakya, Buddha. "Devotional Love in Hinduism." *All You Need to KNow ABout Hinduism*. n.d. http://history-of-hinduism.blogspot.com/2010/10/devotional-love-in-hinduism.html (accessed February 16, 2018).

Sheima. ""Love" in the Quran and Sunnah." *How to Be a Happy Muslim.* July 30, 2016. http://howtobeahappymuslim.com/?p=946 (accessed February 15, 2018).

Shemtov, Rabbi Eliezer. "The Art of Forgiveness." *Chabad.org.* 2018 . http://www.chabad.org/library/article_cdo/aid/1619314/jewish/The-Art-of-Forgiveness.htm (accessed February 19, 2018).

Shermer, Michael. *Heavens on Earth - The Scientific Search for the Afterlife, Immortality, and Utopia.* New York: Henry Holt, 2018.

Shoemaker, H. Stephen. "The Saving of Liberal Christianity." *Shoemaker's Study - the Sermons and Writings of H. Stephen Shoemaker.* n.d. http://shoemakersstudy.com/2018/02/12/the-saving-of-liberal-christianity/ (accessed November 1, 2018).

Siddiqi, Dr. Muzammil H. "Why Does Allah Allow Suffering and Evil in the World?" *Islam Online Archive.* n.d. https://archive.islamonline.net/?p=885 (accessed January 30, 2018).

Slick, Matt. "What is the meaning and purpose of life?" *Christian Apologetics and Research Ministry (CARM).* May 12, 2012. https://carm.org/meaning-of-life (accessed March 27, 2018).

Smith, David Livingstone. *Why We Lie - The Evolutionary Roots of Deception and the Unconscious Mind.* New York: St. Martin's Press, 2004.

Soo Rin Kim - Open Secrets - The price of winning just got higher, especially in the Senate. "The price of winning just got higher, especially in the Senate." *Open Secrets.* Nov 9, 2016. https://www.opensecrets.org/news/2016/11/the-price-of-winning-just-got-higher-especially-in-the-senate/ (accessed May 29, 2020).

Spiritual Excellence. "Happiness in Islam: 5 Steps to a Life of Joy and Purpose." *SpiritualExcellence.* July 2013. http://www.spiritualexcellence.com/blog/happi-ness-in-islam-5-steps-to-a-life-of-joy-and-purpose/ (accessed March 26, 2018).

Staloff, Darren. "Deism and the Founding of the United States." *Divining America, TeacherServe©. National Humanities Center.* May 2, 2020. http://nationalhumaniti-escenter.org/tserve/eighteen/ekeyinfo/deism.htm (accessed May 2, 2020).

Stewart, George. *God and Pain.* New York: Geroge H. Doran Company, 1927.

Story-Fund? "Dunning-Kruger Effect." *Story.Fund.* 2014. http://story.fund/post/114093854037/dunning-kruger-effect (accessed March 19, 2018).

Stöwer, Willy. "Sinking of the RMS Titanic." *Wekimedia Commons.* 1912. By Willy Stöwer, died on 31st May 1931 - Magazine Die Gartenlaube, en:Die Garten-laube and de:Die Gartenlaube, Public Domain, https://commons.wikimedia.org/w/index.php?curid=97646 (accessed August 3, 2019).

"Student Dictionary." *Merriam Webster - Word Central.* 2007. http://wordcentral.com/cgi-bin/student?faith (accessed December 29, 2018).

Subramuniyaswami, Satguru Sivaya. *Dancing with Siva: Hinduism's Contemporary Catechism.* IndiA: Himalayan Academy, 2003.

Sukel, Kayt. *The Art of Risk - The New Science of Courage, Caution, & Chance.* Washing-ton, DC: National Geographic Society, 2016.

Susan C. Imbarrato (Crèvecœur, J. Hector St. John de). "A Library of American Literature: An Anthology in Eleven Volumes. 1891. Vol. III: Literature of the Revolutionary Period, 1765–1787." *Bartleby.com Great Books on-line.* 1782 (Ref 2015). https://www.bartleby.com/400/prose/407.html (accessed May 2, 2020).

Svirsky, Rabbi Efim. "Feeling God's Presence." *Aish.com.* n.d. http://www.aish.com/sp/pg/48894482.html (accessed March 1, 2018).

Taber, I. W. "Moby Dick final chase.jpg." *Wikimedia Commons, the free media repository.* Charles Scribner's Sons, New York. 1902. https://commons.wikimedia.org/w/index.php?curid=11179929 (accessed August 1, 2019).

Ted Johnson - Donald Trump Again Wants To Eliminate Funding For Public Media, But Congress Likely Won't Let Him. "Donald Trump Again Wants To Eliminate Funding For Public Media, But Congress Likely Won't Let Him." *Deadline.* Feb 10, 2020. https://deadline.com/2020/02/donald-trump-public-media-pbs-npr-1202856498/ (accessed May 19, 2020).

Thaler, Richard H., and Cass R. Sunstein. *Nudge - Improving Decision Abou Health, Wealth, and Happiness.* 375 Hudson Street, New York, New York 10014, USA: Penguin Group, 2009.

The Leadership Council On Civil and Human Rights - Trump Administration Civil and Human Rights Rollbacks. "Trump Administration Civil and Human Rights Rollbacks." *The Leadership Council On Civil and Human Rights.* 2020. https://civilrights.org/trump-rollbacks/#2020 (accessed May 30, 2020).

—. "Trump Administration Civil and Human Rights Rollbacks." *The Leadership Council on Civil and Human Right.* 2017. https://civilrights.org/trump-rollbacks/ (accessed May 30, 2020).

The Learning Network. "New York Woman Killed While Witnesses do Nothing." *The Learning Network.* March 13, 2012. https://learning.blogs.nytimes.com/2012/03/13/march-13-1964-new-york-woman-killed-while-witnesses-do-nothing/ (accessed June 19, 2019).

"The Meaning of Life in Buddhism ." *ReligionFacts.com.* November 19, 2016. http://www.religionfacts.com/buddhism/meaning-life (accessed March 27, 2018).

The Week - Don't listen to Paul Ryan: The GOP is still the party of makers and takers. "Don't listen to Paul Ryan: The GOP is still the party of makers and takers." *The Week.* Aug 14, 2014. https://theweek.com/articles/444399/dont-listen-paul-ryan-gop-still-party-makers-takers (accessed May 29, 2020).

Thera, Nyanaponika. "Buddhism and the God-idea." *Buddhist Publication Society - Access to Insight (BCBS Edition).* November 10, 2013. http://www.accesstoinsight.org/lib/authors/nyanaponika/godidea.html (accessed March 1, 2018).

This Day in History(?). "U.S. Constitution ratified." *https://www.history.co.uk/this-day-in-history.* n.d. https://www.history.co.uk/this-day-in-history/21-june/us-constitution-ratified (accessed May 5, 2020).

Thom Hartmann - Does No One Care That 7 Million Votes Were Not Counted? "Does No One Care That 7 Million Votes Were Not Counted?" *Thom Hartmann Program.* Jan 6, 2017. https://www.thomhartmann.com/blog/2017/01/does-no-one-care-7-million-votes-were-not-counted (accessed May 29, 2020).

Turner, Laura Teddy. "Christian Beliefs on the Meaning of Life." *Classroom.* September 17, 2017. https://classroom.synonym.com/christian-beliefs-on-the-meaning-of-life-12087755.html (accessed March 27, 2018).

Tzadok, Ariel Bar. "Prayer for Receiving Divine Guidance (Torah)." *KosherTorah.com.* 2010. http://www.koshertorah.com/PDF/shavuotprayer.pdf (accessed February 9, 2018).

U.S. Department of Health and Human Services. "Leprosy." *Genetics Home Reference.* April 3, 2018. https://ghr.nlm.nih.gov/condition/leprosy (accessed April 9, 2018).

U.S. History - The Peculiar Instution. "27. Peculiar Institution." *U.S. History.org.* 2019. https://www.ushistory.org/us/27.asp (accessed May 27, 2020).

Union of Concerne Scientists - Climate Change and Agriculture. "Climate Change and Agriculture." *Union of Concerne Scientists.* Mar 20, 2019. https://www.ucsusa.org/resources/climate-change-and-agriculture (accessed May 29, 2020).

Unknown. "Sex." *The Buddha's Advice to Laypeople (Guidelines for developing a happier life).* February 8, 2018. https://buddhasadvice.wordpress.com/sex/ (accessed February 12, 2018).

US Census Bureau - Quick Facts. "Quick Facts US." *United States Census Bureau.* n.d. https://www.census.gov/quickfacts/fact/table/US/PST045218 (accessed May 5, 2020).

US Department of Labor - Handy Reference Guide to the Fair Labor Standards Act. "Handy Reference Guide to the Fair Labor Standards Act." *US Department of Labor.* Sep 2016. https://www.dol.gov/agencies/whd/compliance-assistance/handy-reference-guide-flsa (accessed May 7, 2020).

US Government. *All Types of STDs and STIs, STD Symptoms, STD Pictures, STD Treatment.* July 20,, 2015. http://www.std-gov.org/blog/types-of-stds/ (accessed November 4, 2016).

V, Jayaram. "Ananda, the State of Bliss or Happiness." *Hinduwebsite.com.* n.d. http://www.hinduwebsite.com/hinduism/concepts/ananda.asp (accessed March 26, 2018).

—. "Death and Afterlife in Hinduism." *Hinduwebsite.com.* n.d. http://www.hinduwebsite.com/hinduism/h_death.asp (accessed March 2, 2018).

—. "Good and Evil in Hinduism." *Hinduwebsite.com.* n.d. http://www.hinduwebsite.com/hinduism/h_goodandevil.asp (accessed February 9, 2018).

—. *Introduction to Hinduism.* Pure LIfe Vision, 2012.

—. "The 24 Tattvas of Creation in Samkhya Darshana." *Hinduwebsite.com.* n.d. The 24 Tattvas of Creation in Samkhya Darshana (accessed March 19, 2018).

—. "The Abiding Principles of Hindu Dharma." *Hinduwebsite.com.* n.d. https://www.hinduwebsite.com/what-is-hindu-dharma.asp (accessed October 28, 2018).

—. "What is Faith? Faith in Hinduism." *Induwebsite.com.* n.d. http://www.hinduwebsite.com/faith.asp (accessed March 19, 2018).

Van Loon, Hendrik. *Tolerance - The Story of Man's Struggle for the Right to Think.* New York: Liveright Publishing Corp, 1927 Revised 1940.

Vance, J.D. *Hillbilly Elegy - A Memoir of a Family and Culture in Crisis.* New York: HarperCollins, 2016.

Vesconte, Pietro - British Library, Public Domain. "Early World Maps." *Wikipedia.* 1321. https://commons.wikimedia.org/w/index.php?curid=3595637 (accessed November 8, 2016).

Vidyamala. "Being here: A Buddhist approach to pain." *Wildmind Buddhist Meditation.* February 20, 2007. https://www.wildmind.org/applied/pain/being-here (accessed January 30, 2018).

Vij, Rajiv. "Maslow's Hierarchy Revisited…the Eastern Way!" *Personal Alchemy Blog.* October 11, 2011. https://rajivvij.com/2008/09/maslows-hierarchy-revisitedthe-eastern.html (accessed November 26, 2018).

Wakefield, Dan. *How Do We Know When It's God?* Boston, New York, London: Little, Brown and Company, 1999.

Waldinge, Robert. "What makes a good life? Lessons from the longest study on happiness." *TED.* January 25, 2016. https://www.youtube.com/watch?v=8KkKuTCFvzI (accessed November 20, 2018).

Waldinger, Robert. "What makes a good life? Lessons from the longest study on happiness." *TED.* January 25, 2016. https://www.youtube.com/watch?v=8KkKuTCFvzI (accessed December 13, 2018).

Watson, Peter. *The Age of Atheists - How we have sought to live since the deth of God.* New York: Simon & Schuster, 2014.

Weinberg, Rabbi Noah. "The Meaning Of Life." *Aish.com.* n.d. http://www.aish.com/sp/f/48964356.html (accessed March 27, 2018).

Weiner-Davis, Michele. "The sex-starved marriage ." *TEDxCU.* April 14, 2014. https://www.youtube.com/watch?v=Ep2MAx95m20 (accessed December 12, 2018).

Wellman, Jack. "Top 7 Bible Verses About Curiosity." *Patheos.* November 28, 2016. http://www.patheos.com/blogs/christiancrier/2016/11/28/top-7-bible-verses-about-curiosity/ (accessed June 12, 2018).

Westerville Public Library - Anti-Saloon League Museum. "Anti-Saloon League Museum." *Westerville Public Library.* n.d. http://www.westervillelibrary.org/AntiSaloon/ (accessed May 8, 2020).

Weston, Walter L. *The Self-Healing Pocket Guide.* Wadsworth, Ohio: Transitions Press, 1996.

"What is Islam?" *Inspired by Mohammad.com.* 2010? http://www.inspiredbymuhammad.com/islam.php?&content_80=2#10 (accessed March 27, 2018).

"What is the Purpose of Life in Buddhism." *Teachings of the Buddha.* n.d. https://teachingsofthebuddha.com/what-is-the-purpose-of-life-in-buddhism/ (accessed March 27, 2018).

Wiesner, Irving. "A Jewish Psychiatrist's Views on the Meaning of Life." *Jews for Jesus.* April 1, 2006. https://jewsforjesus.org/publications/issues/issues-v16-n06/ajewish-psychiatrist-s-views-on-the-meaning-of-life/ (accessed March 27, 2018).

Wikipedia - Abolish ICE. "Abolish ICE." *Wikipedia.* May 16, 2020. https://en.wikipedia.org/wiki/Abolish_ICE (accessed May 30, 2020).

Wikipedia - Annuit coeptis. "Annuit coeptis." *Wikipedia.* May 1, 2020. https://en.wikipedia.org/wiki/Annuit_c%C5%93ptis (accessed May 18, 2020).

Wikipedia - Buffett Rule. "Buffett Rule." *Buffett Rule.* Oct 25, 2019. https://en.wikipedia.org/wiki/Buffett_Rule (accessed May 30, 2020).

Wikipedia - Bush v Gore. "Bush v Gore." *Wikipedia.* May 14, 2020. https://en.wikipedia.org/wiki/Bush_v._Gore (accessed Jun 1, 2020).

Wikipedia - Campaign finance in the United States. "Campaign finance in the United States." *Wikipedia.* May 21, 2020. https://en.wikipedia.org/wiki/Campaign_finance_in_the_United_States (accessed May 29, 2020).

Wikipedia - E pluribus unum. "E pluribus unum." *Wikipedia.* May 14, 2020. https://en.wikipedia.org/wiki/E_pluribus_unum (accessed May 18, 2020).

Wikipedia - Eighteenth Amendment to the United States Constitution. "Eighteenth Amendment to the United States Constitution." *Wikipedia.* May 6, 2020. https://en.wikipedia.org/wiki/Eighteenth_Amendment_to_the_United_States_Constitution (accessed May 8, 2020).

Wikipedia - English Americans. "English Americans." *Wikipedia.* Apr 24, 2020. https://en.wikipedia.org/wiki/English_Americans#Census:_1980-2000 (accessed May 1, 2020).

Wikipedia - FCC fairness doctrine. "FCC fairness doctrine." *Wikipedia.* Apr 30, 2020. https://en.wikipedia.org/wiki/FCC_fairness_doctrine#Basic_doctrine (accessed May 22, 2020).

Wikipedia - German American. "German Americans." *Wikipedia.* Apr 29, 2020. https://en.wikipedia.org/wiki/German_Americans (accessed May 1, 2020).

Wikipedia - In God We Trust. "In God We Trust." *Wikipedia.* May 18, 2020. https://en.wikipedia.org/wiki/In_God_We_Trust (accessed May 18, 2020).

—. "In God We Trust." *Wikipedia.* May 21, 2020. https://en.wikipedia.org/wiki/In_God_We_Trust (accessed May 25, 2020).

Wikipedia - Irish Americans. "Irish-Americans." *Wikipedia.* Apr 16, 2020. https://en.wikipedia.org/wiki/Irish_Americans (accessed May 1, 2020).

Wikipedia - Jefferson Bible. "Jefferson Bible." *Wikipedia.* March 19, 2020. https://en.wikipedia.org/wiki/Jefferson_Bible (accessed May 2, 2020).

Wikipedia - List of U.S. states by population. "List of U.S. states by population." *Wikipedia.* May 5, 2020. https://simple.wikipedia.org/wiki/List_of_U.S._states_by_population (accessed May 29, 2020).

Wikipedia - Manifest Destiny. "Manifest Destiny." *Wikipedia.* Apr 25, 2020. https://en.wikipedia.org/wiki/Manifest_destiny (accessed May 2, 2020).

Wikipedia - Monroe Doctrine. "Monroe Doctrine." *Wikipedia.* Apr 28, 2020. https://en.wikipedia.org/wiki/Monroe_Doctrine (accessed May 2, 2020).

Wikipedia - Native Americans in the United States. "Native Americans in the United States." *Wikipedia.* May 17, 2020. https://en.wikipedia.org/wiki/Native_Americans_in_the_United_States (accessed May 18, 2020).

Wikipedia - No Surrender (Song). "No Surrender (Song)." *Wikipedia.* Apr 20, 2020. https://en.wikipedia.org/wiki/No_Surrender_%28song%29 (accessed May 30, 2020).

Wikipedia - Novus ordo seclorum. "Novus oro seclorum." *Wikipedia.* May 1, 2020. https://en.wikipedia.org/wiki/Novus_ordo_seclorum (accessed May 18, 2020).

Wikipedia - Racial and ethnic categories. "Racial and ethnic categories." *Wikipedia.* May 14, 2020. https://en.wikipedia.org/wiki/Race_and_ethnicity_in_the_United_States (accessed May 18, 2020).

Wikipedia - T.T Ross - "Let the World Go Away". "T.T. Ross." *Wikipedia.* Mar 22, 2020. https://en.wikipedia.org/wiki/T.T._Ross (accessed May 27, 2020).

Wikipedia - United States congressional apportionment. "United States congressional apportionment." *Wikipedia.* May 15, 2020. https://en.wikipedia.org/wiki/United_States_congressional_apportionment (accessed May 29, 2020).

Wikipedia - United States immigration statistics. "United States immigration statistics." *Wikipedia*. Apr 10, 2020. https://en.wikipedia.org/wiki/United_States_immigration_statistics (accessed May 1, 2020).

Wikipedia - United States presidential elections in which the winner lost the popular vote. "United States presidential elections in which the winner lost the popular vote." *Wikipedia*. May 30, 2020. https://en.wikipedia.org/w/index.php?title=United_States_presidential_elections_in_which_the_winner_lost_the_popular_vote&action=history (accessed Jun 1, 2020).

Wikipedia. "Buddhist vegetarianism." *Wikipedia*. November 29, 2018. https://en.wikipedia.org/wiki/Buddhist_vegetarianism (accessed February 5, 2019).

—. "Diet in Hinduism." *Wikipedia*. January 31, 2019. https://en.wikipedia.org/wiki/Diet_in_Hinduism (accessed February 5, 2019).

—. "Eternal Sin." *Wikipedia*. August 17, 2018. https://en.wikipedia.org/wiki/Eternal_sin (accessed September 27, 2018).

—. "List of Christian denominations by number of members." *Wikipedia*. August 20, 2018. https://simple.wikipedia.org/wiki/List_of_Christian_denominations_by_number_of_members#Catholic_Church_-_1 (accessed December 28, 2018).

—. "List of religious populations." *Wikipedia*. February 5, 2018. https://en.wikipedia.org/wiki/List_of_religious_populations (accessed February 13, 2018).

—. "Old Testament." *Wikipedia*. n.d. https://en.wikipedia.org/wiki/Old_Testament (accessed October 15, 2018).

—. "Quran." *Wikipedia*. n.d. https://en.wikipedia.org/wiki/Quran (accessed October 16 2018).

—. "Religous Views on Love." *Wikpedia*. November 10, 2017. https://en.wikipedia.org/wiki/Religious_views_on_love#Hindu (accessed February 16, 2018).

—. "Synoptic Gospels - Wikipedia." *Wikipedia*. n.d. https://www.google.com/imgres?imgurl=https://upload.wikimedia.org/wikipedia/commons/thumb/6/6f/Relationship_between_synoptic_gospels-en.svg/360px-Relationship_between_synoptic_gospels-en.svg.png&imgrefurl=https://en.wikipedia.org/wiki/Synoptic_Gospels&h=4 (accessed October 12, 2018).

—. "Tanmatras." *Wikipedia*. September 26, 2016. https://en.wikipedia.org/wiki/Tanmatras (accessed April 11, 2019).

—. "Two Gospel Hypothesis." *Wikipedia*. n.d. https://www.google.com/imgres?imgurl=https://upload.wikimedia.org/wikipedia/commons/thumb/e/ee/Synoptic_problem_two_source_colored.png/220px-Synoptic_problem_two_source_colored.png&imgrefurl=https://en.wikipedia.org/wiki/Two-source_hypothesis&h=257&w=220& (accessed November 11, 2016).

Wikiquote - Grover Norquist. "Grover Norquist." *Wikiquote*. May 13, 2019. https://en.wikiquote.org/w/index.php?title=Grover_Norquist&action=history (accessed May 19, 2020).

Wilber, Ken. *The Religion of Tomorrow*. Boulder: Shambhala Publications, 2018.

Wilder, Thornton. *Our Town*. 1938 Book 1940 Movie.

Willett, Sunder. "Evil and Theodicy in Hinduism." *Denison Journal of Religion (Vol 14, Article 5)*. 2015. https://digitalcommons.denison.edu/cgi/viewcontent.cgi?referer=https://www.google.com/&httpsredir=1&article=1095&context=religion (accessed February 9, 2018)

Winkler, Rabbi Gershon. "What Does Judaism Say About Love? pg 24." *Ask the Rabbis*. September-October 2010. http://www.momentmag.com/wp-content/uploads/2013/02/What-Does-Judaism-Say-About-Love.pdf (accessed February 13, 2018).

World Populatioin Review - Africa. "Africa." *World Population Review*. 2020. https://worldpopulationreview.com/continents/africa-population/ (accessed May 31, 2020).

World Population Review - Central America and South America. "Central America and South America." *World Population Review*. 2020. https://worldpopulationreview.com/continents/south-america-population/ (accessed May 31, 2020).

Worldometer - Population of Italy. "Population of Italy." *worldometer*. May 27, 2020. https://www.worldometers.info/world-population/italy-population/ (accessed May 27, 2020).

Worldometer. "UK Population." *Worldodometer*. 2020. https://www.worldometers.info/world-population/uk-population/ (accessed May 1, 2020).

About the Author

Ivan Beggs

Ivan Beggs has lived, worked, and traveled in the US, Europe, India, China, Vietnam, and South America. He retired from The Timken Company with the position of Program Manager and from the US Army Reserves with the rank of Colonel, with two Bronze Stars and a Legion of Merit.

He attempts to understand why people believe what they do. So, he is open to conversation about the book and is willing to change the statements. Feel free to contact him as guests in each other's lives at:

Quest4a@protonmail.com

Education:

- Brooklyn Technical High School
- BS, Worcester Polytechnic Institute
- MA, Theology, Trinity Lutheran Seminary
- MS, Ohio State University
- MBA, Ohio State University
- Graduate US Army War College.

Married with four children, four grandchildren. Lives in Hendersonville, North Carolina.